LUMENARC
ENTERPRISES

Why Didn't You tell me Before?

Why Didn’t You tell me Before?

Jose Rosario

Why Didn't You tell me Before?

ISBN: 978-1-969803-04-8

Disclaimer

The information, figures, and examples presented in this book are intended solely for educational purposes to illustrate fundamental financial concepts and tools. They are not intended as specific financial or legal advice, quotes, estimates, or recommendations related to any company, product, or investment opportunity. This book is not a solicitation or sale of any service or product. The only intention is to educate society and help prepare for a better future. Readers should understand that the numbers used are hypothetical and simplified to aid comprehension and do not reflect real-world data. This book aims to provide a foundational academic understanding of financial literacy, and readers are encouraged to seek personalized advice from qualified financial professionals before making any financial decisions.

Content

Introduction: Why Didn't You Tell Me Before?

This is a question I've heard countless times. It's always from incredibly hardworking people, full of potential but lacking one thing: the right tools and knowledge to manage their finances. You see, I've learned a lot of lessons the hard way, and it breaks my heart when others have to make the same mistakes. That's why this book exists to help you avoid those pitfalls. But first, let me ask you something: You've probably been told to read many great books about personal finance, right?

Maybe you've even bought a few that are now collecting dust on your shelf (we've all been there). So why should you read THIS book first? Here is the challenge; most financial books assume you already speak "*money language.*" They throw around terms like "*compound interest,*" "*asset allocation,*" and "*diversification*" like you grew up in a Wall Street boardroom. This book? It's different. Think of it as your financial translator, turning all that confusing jargon into simple, actionable steps you can start using today. This is the book you read BEFORE you dive into the deep end of the financial pool. Consider it your financial life jacket.

We've all had that moment, right? You're going along in life, trying to manage everything; working, paying bills, maybe saving a little here and there, and then something happens. Something big. A surprise bill, a financial mistake, or just the realization that you're not as prepared as you thought. And suddenly, the question hits you: "*Why didn't someone tell me about this before?*"

I remember when I started my first real job. Man, I felt like I was on top of the world! I had visions of finally being able to afford all the things I'd been dreaming about. I was ready to conquer the world with my shiny new paycheck. But then reality hit harder than a Monday morning alarm clock. Taxes, insurance, student loans, credit scores; things I had never really understood before. It was like I had missed an entire semester of "*Adult Life 101*" and was suddenly expected to ace the final exam. That's when I asked myself the same question: "*Why didn't anyone tell me this before?*"

And here's the kicker, I wasn't alone. I started talking to friends, colleagues, even my family, and guess what? We were all fumbling around in the dark, pretending we knew what we were doing. It was like we were all part of some unspoken conspiracy to act like we understood money while secretly Googling "*What is a 401k?*" at 2 AM.

That's what inspired me to write this book. Because I've seen it time and again; smart, ambitious people who want to do the right thing, but they've just never been given the tools to succeed in the financial world. Maybe you're one of them. Maybe you've been working for a while but don't really know how to budget, or maybe you're someone who just started their career and is trying to make sense of a completely new system. We have all felt lost on the road, and the GPS has let us down. This book will help you understand the basics of financial tools to avoid common pitfalls in your personal finances. Hopefully quicker than the GPS telling you to take the next exit on the right while you're in the farthest left lane.

So, let me tell you what I wish I had known when I started out. And here's the thing: learning about money doesn't need to be complicated. I know it feels overwhelming sometimes, like trying to solve a Rubik's cube while riding a unicycle, but trust me, with just a little bit of knowledge, you can start making better decisions and taking control of your financial future.

Take credit cards, for example. I remember the first time I got approved for one. It felt like I'd just been handed a magic wand that could make all my wants disappear (temporarily, of course). But here's what I learned the hard way: credit cards are like power tools, incredibly useful when used strategically, but potentially Dangerous if you don't know what you're doing. They are not a trap by themselves, but they can become one if you don't use them strategically. It's like having a chainsaw in the right hands, it's a valuable tool; in the wrong hands, well, let's just say things can get messy fast.

If I had known that back then, if someone had explained that credit cards are essentially borrowing (loans) with additional cost, AKA interest rate, that can make your head spin; I would have avoided so many sleepless nights and that sinking feeling every time I opened my credit card statement. Or take saving for the future. It sounds like a far-off goal, right? Something for "*Future You*" to worry about. But I wish someone had told me just how powerful the habit of saving is, even when it feels impossible. Even saving what feels like pocket change can make a huge difference, especially when you start early. I used to think, "*What's the point of saving $25 a month when I have bills to pay?*" But $25 a month might not buy you a fancy dinner, but over time, it can buy you something much more valuable: peace of mind.

When I first started working, I had no idea where my money was going. It was like my paycheck had developed legs and was running away from me. One day I'd feel rich, and the next, I'd be doing that awkward Dance we all know; checking my bank balance three times before buying a coffee, to make sure I could afford it. I found myself aware of expenses just when I had to make a payment. However, once I understood how to budget properly, track my income and expenses, and prioritize my spending, everything changed.

Suddenly, I was the one calling the shots, not my bills. Suddenly, I wasn't asking "*Why didn't I know this before?*" I was living the answers I needed. This book isn't about throwing a bunch of financial terms at you that sound like they belong in a foreign language dictionary. It's about making these concepts simple and practical. I'll show you what you need to know, how you can start using it today, and why these lessons will make a real difference in your life. Think of me as your financial GPS; I'll help you navigate from "*financially confused*" to "*financially confident*" without taking any unnecessary detours through Stress-ville. I'll break it down for you, step by step, and show you how even small changes in your money habits can lead to big rewards in the future. We're talking about simple tweaks that can transform your relationship with money from "*It's complicated*" to "*We're in a healthy, committed relationship.*"

Whether you're just starting your career. navigating a new job, or simply trying to understand how to make your money work for you instead of against you, this book will be your guide. It's not just about surviving the financial world, it's about thriving in it. And trust me, once you start applying these tips, you'll be the one people come to asking, "*Why didn't you tell me this before?*"

So, buckle up, grab your favorite beverage, and let's turn you into the financially savvy person you were meant to be. Your future self will thank you for it.

Chapter 1: Credit — Not Free Money, My Friend

Here's the truth bomb: Credit isn't magic, and it's definitely not free money. But, and this is a big but, if you learn how to handle credit right, it can be your financial best friend. Think of it like adopting a German Shepherd puppy. Train it well from the start, and you'll have a loyal companion that protects your house and impresses your neighbors. Ignore its training, and you might come home to find your favorite shoes have been turned into expensive chew toys. So, let's get to know this financial "*puppy*" called credit.

Welcome to the wild world of credit! If you're just starting your financial journey or feeling like everyone else got a secret manual on how money works (spoiler: they didn't), you might be wondering: What on earth is credit, and why does everyone talk about it like it's some kind of mystical financial unicorn?

What Is Credit? (Hint: It's Not Free Money)

Credit is when someone, like a bank, credit card company, or that one friend who always has cash, lends you money today, and you promise to pay it back later, usually with some extra money called interest. Think of interest as a "*thank you*" fee for letting you borrow their cash.

It's like borrowing your friend's car for the weekend. You get to use it now, but you promise to return it with a full tank of gas as a thank you. The gas money? That's your interest payment.

Here is what credit is NOT: A gift card from your fairy godmother. It's a loan, plain and simple.

You use credit to:

- ✓ Buy things you can't pay for all at once (like a car, house, or that laptop that's definitely "for school.")
- ✓ Cover emergencies (emphasis on "emergencies"—your daily coffee habit doesn't count.)
- ✓ Build a history that shows you're trustworthy with money (like getting financial street cred.)

However, treat credit like free money, and watch the chaos unfold:

- × You could get stuck in debt for years (welcome to the hamster wheel of minimum payments)
- × You'll pay way more than the original price tag

× You'll develop a stress-induced eye twitch every time you check your balance

Real Talk Example:

Imagine you buy a $1,000 phone on your credit card because you need that fancy new camera for your "*photography hobby*" (a.k.a. Instagram pics). If you only make the minimum payments each month, by the time you finally pay it off, you could end up spending $1,400 or more due to interest. That's an extra $400 just for the same ugly selfies your old phone could've taken. Not such a great deal after all, huh?

Your Credit Score: The Financial Report Card You Can't Hide from Your Parents

Your credit score is like your financial report card, except this one follows you around for life, and you can't forge your parents' signature to make it go away. It answers the burning question: "*Can this person be trusted to pay back money, or are they going to disappear into the night like a financial ghost?*"

Credit scores range from 300 (basically financial kryptonite) to 850 (financial superhero status). Here's the breakdown:

800-850: You're basically the financial equivalent of a golden retriever, everyone loves you

740-799: Solid, dependable, gets invited to all the good loan parties

670-739: Average, but hey, average gets the job done

580-669: You're in the "prove yourself" zone

300-579: Time for some serious credit CPR

Better scores mean better deals:

- ✓ Lower interest rates (save thousands on big purchases)
- ✓ Easier approvals for loans and credit cards (increase your purchase power)
- ✓ Sometimes cheaper car insurance or better rental terms (lower your expenses)
- ✓ Landlords actually want to rent to you (revolutionary concept!)

What Makes Up Your Credit Score? (The Secret Recipe Revealed)

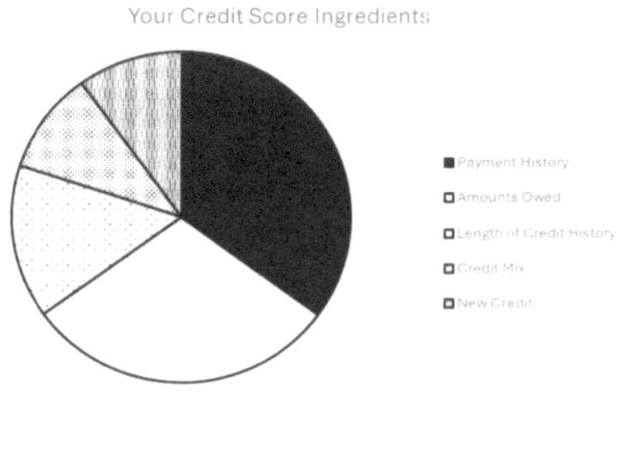

Think of your credit score like a secret sauce recipe. Here are the ingredients:

- **35% Payment History:** Do you pay your bills on time? This is the biggest slice of the pie, so don't mess it up. Even being late once can ding your score.
- **30% Amounts Owed:** How much of your available credit are you using? Using 90% of your credit limit is like showing up to a marathon having already run 20 miles; technically possible, but not recommended.
- **15% Length of Credit History:** How long have you had credit? Time is your friend here. Keep your oldest credit card, even if it's uglier than your high school yearbook photo.
- **10% Credit Mix:** Different types of credit, like cards and loans. Think of it as having a balanced diet; you want variety, but you don't need to try every single financial product on the menu.
- **10% New Credit:** How often you apply for new credit. Opening five credit cards in one week is like speed dating; desperate and likely to end badly.

Why Does Credit Matter? (Plot Twist: It Matters More Than You Think)

Here is where it gets real: Your credit score is basically your financial reputation, and in today's world, your reputation gets around faster than gossip in a small town.

Landlords peek at your credit report like they're stalking your social media. Bad credit can mean getting rejected for that perfect apartment, or worse, having to pay deposits that make you question your life choices.

Banks use your credit score to decide whether to lend you money and at what interest rate. The difference between good and bad credit on a car loan can literally be thousands of dollars. That's a lot of fancy coffee money.

Sometimes even employers check your credit, especially for jobs involving money. They do this because your financial responsibility can reflect how seriously you take important matters. Employers want to hire people who demonstrate responsibility and reliability.

Real-world example:

Let's say you want to buy a $20,000 car. With excellent credit, you might get a 3% interest rate. With poor credit, you might get stuck with 24%. Over five years, that's the difference between paying $22,000 total versus $35,000. That's $13,000 extra, enough to buy another (smaller) car!

	Excellent Credit	Poor Credit
Loan amount	20,000	20,000
Term	60	60
Interest rate	3%	24%
Monthly payment	$359	$575
Total loan interest	$1,562	$14,521
Total paid	**$21,562**	**$34,521**

That is:

✓ **With excellent credit (3% interest):**

Total paid over 5 years ≈ $22,000

× **With poor credit (24% interest):**

Total paid over 5 years ≈ $35,000

That's $13,000 extra, enough to buy a whole second (used) car just because of your credit score! Congratulations, you just paid for two cars while only getting one!

What is the APR (Annual Percentage Rate)?

Do you remember the $1,000 cellphone that ended up being a $1,400 cellphone? The APR will help you estimate how much more you will end paying over time In detail, the Annual Percentage Rate (APR) is the total cost of borrowing money, expressed as a yearly interest rate. It includes not just the interest you pay on the loan, but also any additional fees or costs associated with borrowing. The idea behind APR is to give you a clearer picture of how much a loan will cost you over the course of a year, allowing you to compare different loan offers more easily.

For example, if you borrow money with a 10% APR, you're paying 10% of the loan amount in interest and fees each year. So, for a loan of $1,000, you'd pay $100 in interest and fees annually.

APR is a helpful tool because it combines all costs into one number, which makes it easier to compare different loans, credit cards, or mortgages. It helps you understand the true cost of borrowing, including any hidden fees, and how much you'll actually be paying over time.

How to Train Your Credit Dog (Without Getting Bitten)

Here are some simple, life-changing habits to keep your credit score happy:

- ✓ **Pay your bills on time—every time.** Set up automatic payments if you have to. Your future self will thank you, and your credit score will love you.
- ✓ **Keep your credit card balances low.** Aim for using less than 30% of your credit limit. If your limit is $1,000, try to keep your balance under $300. Think of it as leaving room for dessert.
- ✓ **Don't apply for credit like you're collecting trading cards.** Each application can temporarily lower your

score. Space them out like you're rationing your favorite snacks.

✓ **Check your credit report once a year.** It's free (seriously, free!), and you might catch errors. Finding a mistake on your credit report is like finding money in your old jeans; surprisingly common and always exciting.

✓ **Don't close your oldest credit card.** Even if it's that ugly card from when you were 18 and thought neon green was a good color choice. Age matters in the credit world.

The $5,000 Credit Limit Trap (Don't Be This Guy)

Let me tell you about my friend Dan. Dan got his first credit card with a $5,000 limit and thought, "*Sweet! The bank just gave me $5,000 to spend!*" So, he went on a shopping spree that would make a reality TV star jealous; new clothes, gadgets, dinners out, you name it.

Fast forward six months, and Dan was making minimum payments on a maxed-out card, watching his balance grow like a chia pet from hell. The interest was eating him alive, and he started calling it his "*forever loan*" because it felt like he'd never pay it off.

The lesson? A credit limit isn't a spending target, it's a ceiling. Just because you CAN max out your card doesn't mean you SHOULD. It's like having a speed limit of 70 mph; you don't have to drive 70 mph everywhere you go.

The Millionaire, The Fancy Car, and the Manhattan Bank: A Credit Lesson That'll Blow Your Mind

Here is a story, from an unknown author, that perfectly illustrates how credit can work for you when you truly understand it:

A multi-millionaire walks into a fancy Manhattan bank (think marble floors, intimidating security guards, and loan officers who look like they iron their business cards). He asks for a tiny loan, just $5,000. The loan officer, probably wondering if this is some kind of prank, asks for collateral, something of value to hold as guarantee if he didn't pay. The millionaire casually tosses over the keys to a $200,000 Ferrari parked outside.

The bank employees are trying not to laugh. Here's this wealthy guy using a Ferrari as collateral for a $5,000 loan. But hey, business is business, so they process the loan and park the car in their secure garage. Two weeks later, the millionaire returns, pays back the $5,000 plus about $20 in interest, and walks away with his Ferrari keys. The curious loan officer ask, "*Sir, why did you borrow such a small amount when you clearly have plenty of money?*" The millionaire grins and says, "*Where else in Manhattan can I park my car safely for two weeks for just twenty bucks?*"

The lesson:

Credit is a tool. When you understand how it works, you can use it to solve problems in creative ways. The millionaire didn't need the money, he needed the parking space. He used credit strategically to get what he actually wanted.

Pro Tips That'll Make You Look Like a Credit Genius

Treat your credit card like a debit card. If you don't have the money to pay it off this month, don't buy it. This simple rule will save you from 90% of credit card disasters.

1. **Use the "24-hour rule" for big purchases.** Sleep on it. If you still want it tomorrow, and you can afford it, go for it. You'll be amazed how many "*must-have*" items suddenly become "*eh, never mind*" after a good night's sleep.
2. **Set up balance alerts.** Most credit card companies will text you when you're approaching your limit. It's like having a financial babysitter.
3. **Pay more than the minimum.** Even paying an extra $25 a month can save you hundreds in interest and years of payments.

Bottom Line: Credit Is Your Financial Sidekick

Credit is a tool, like a smartphone or a car. Used well, it helps you build a better life, achieve your goals, and create opportunities. Used badly, it can chain you down faster than you can say "*minimum payment.*"

So, treat your credit like that German Shepherd puppy we talked about earlier: train it well with consistent, responsible habits, and it'll protect your financial future for life. Ignore it, and you might just get bitten by debt, high interest rates, and missed opportunities.

Remember: You're not just building credit, you're building your financial reputation. And in a world where your reputation can open doors or slam them shut, you want to make sure yours is opening the right ones. Ready to start training your credit dog? Your future self is counting on you. Let's make them proud!

Chapter 2: Your Consumer Reports — Your Money Reputation

"Your financial life leaves footprints. Reports show where you've been... and where you're going."

Introduction: The Story Behind Your Money Reputation

Picture this: You're walking through life, and every financial decision you make is like leaving a footprint in wet cement. Some footprints are perfectly shaped; neat, clean, and heading in the right direction. Others? Well, let's just say they look like you were Dancing in a thunderstorm while wearing clown shoes.

Now imagine that banks, landlords, employers, and insurance companies are like financial detectives with magnifying glasses, examining every single one of your footprints. They're not being nosy, they're trying to figure out if you're the kind of person who pays their bills or the kind who "*forgets*" about them until the lights get shut off.

These footprints are called consumer reports, and they're basically your financial biography written by companies you've probably never heard of. But here's the thing: just like you wouldn't want someone spreading rumors about you at school or work, you don't want these reports telling lies about your money habits. Don't worry though! By the end of this chapter, you'll know exactly how to keep your financial reputation cleaner than your mom's kitchen counters.

What Is a Consumer Report, Anyway?

Okay, imagine you're at a job interview, and instead of just asking about your experience, the interviewer pulls out a thick file with your name on it. Inside, they've got details about every apartment you've ever lived in, every bill you've ever paid late, and that time you bounced a check because you forgot to transfer money from savings. Creepy? Maybe. Reality? Absolutely.

A consumer report is any report about YOU that companies use to decide if they want to do business with you. It's like having a permanent record that follows you around, except instead of detention slips, it's filled with financial information.

Here's what these reports can include:

- ✓ Your credit history—Every credit card, loan, and payment you've ever made (or missed)
- ✓ Your payment history—Whether you're the "always on time" person or the "I'll pay it eventually" person
- ✓ Public records—Court judgments, liens, bankruptcies (basically, your legal financial drama)
- ✓ Criminal background—Some jobs check this too (yes, that parking ticket might show up)
- ✓ Insurance claims — That time you backed into a mailbox? Yeah, they know about it
- ✓ Employment history—Past jobs, education, and probably that summer you worked at the ice cream shop
- ✓ Addresses—Every place you've lived, like a timeline of your life choices

So basically, your consumer report is your entire financial life story, except you didn't get to write it yourself.

Why Should You Care About This Money Reputation?

Here's the brutal truth: Companies don't know you personally. They can't call your mom and ask, "*Hey, is Dan responsible with money?*" (Though if they did, she'd probably say, " *Well, he did lose his lunch money three times in second grade, but he's improved since then!*")

Instead, companies check your consumer reports to answer the million-dollar questions:

- Can they trust you with a loan, or are you going to disappear like a magician's rabbit?
- Should they rent you that apartment, or will you turn it into a circus?
- Will you pay your bills on time, or do they need to start a collection agency?
- Should they hire you, or are you going to embezzle the coffee fund?
- What insurance price should they give you—the "responsible citizen" rate or the "walking zombie" rate?

Think of your consumer reports as your financial dating profile. You want it to say "*stable, reliable, great with money*" instead of "*hot mess, avoid at all costs.*"

Consumer Reports

Credit Report
ChexSystems Report
Employment Screening Reports

The Most Famous Consumer Report: The Credit Report

When most people say, "*I need to check my credit,*" they're talking about the credit report; the Beyoncé of consumer reports. Everyone knows about it, everyone talks about it, and it has the power to make or break your financial dreams.

Credit reports come from three big companies called credit bureaus (they're like the three wise men of credit, except they're not particularly wise, and they definitely don't bring gifts):

The Big Three:

1. Equifax (probably has your info on file)
2. Experian (definitely has your info on file)
3. TransUnion (100% has your info on file)

These companies are like financial paparazzi; they follow you around, taking notes on everything you do with money. Here's what you'll find on a credit report:

- Your credit cards and loans (every single one you've ever had)
- Balances and limits (how much you owe vs. how much you could spend)

- Payment history (the good, the bad, and the "oops, I forgot")
- How long you've had accounts (credit age matters, like fine wine)
- Any bankruptcies or serious financial trouble (the stuff you'd rather forget)
- Who has checked your credit report (yes, they keep track of who's been snooping)

It's basically your financial report card that follows you everywhere, except you can't hide it from your parents or forge their signature on it.

How Lenders Use Your Credit Report (Spoiler: They're Judging You)

Lenders are like that friend who always asks to borrow money but never pays it back, except they're the ones with the money, and they're being super careful about who they lend it to. They read your credit report like they're studying for the most important test of their lives.

They want to know:

- Can you handle a new loan without having a financial meltdown?
- Are you likely to pay back what you borrow, or are you going to ghost them like a bad Tinder date?

- Are you the financial equivalent of a golden retriever (loyal and trustworthy) or a cat (unpredictable and likely to knock things off the table)?

A clean credit report says:

"This person is responsible, pays their bills on time, and probably flosses regularly."

A messy credit report says:

"This person might pay us back... eventually... maybe... if we're lucky."

It's like when you lend your car to a friend. If they return it with a full tank of gas and no mysterious dents, you'd probably lend it again. If they return it three weeks late with an empty tank and a collection of parking tickets, you might suddenly develop "*car lending amnesia.*"

But Wait... There's More Than Just Credit Reports!

Surprise! Credit reports are just the tip of the iceberg. There's a whole underwater world of consumer reports that companies use to judge your financial worthiness. It's like discovering there's not just one social media platform keeping track of your life, but several.

LexisNexis Consumer Report: The Sherlock Holmes of Financial Data

LexisNexis is like that friend who remembers everything you've ever done and brings it up at the worst possible moments. They track:

- Your addresses over time (every place you've lived since you were 18)
- Past landlords (and whether you left on good terms or not)
- Judgments or liens (court decisions about money you owe)
- Insurance claims (that fender bender from three years ago)
- Public records (basically, your entire legal financial history)
- Who uses LexisNexis reports?
- Insurance companies looking for red flags
- Landlords checking if you're a nightmare tenant
- Lenders who want to dig deeper than your credit report

Think of LexisNexis as the detective who can piece together your entire financial story from seemingly random clues. They're really good at their job, which is either impressive or terrifying, depending on your perspective.

ChexSystems Report: The Bank Account Bouncer

ChexSystems is like the bouncer at an exclusive club, except the club is "*people who can open bank accounts.*" They focus specifically on your banking history:

- Overdrafts (when you spent more money than you had, whoops!)
- Closed accounts (especially ones closed for cause)
- Fraud flags (if someone thought you were up to no good)
- Unpaid fees (those $35 overdraft fees add up fast)

Banks use ChexSystems reports to decide if they want to let you open a checking account. If you've had banking problems before, ChexSystems remembers, and they're not shy about telling everyone.

Real-world example:

My friend Sarah overdrafted her checking account multiple times in college (ramen noodles and textbooks don't budget themselves), and when she tried to open a new account after graduation, three different banks turned her down because of her ChexSystems report. She had to use a prepaid debit card for six months until the negative information aged off her report.

Employment Background Reports: Your Professional Biography

Some employers run background checks before hiring, especially for jobs involving money, security, or trust. They might look at:

- Criminal history (including those parking tickets you thought nobody cared about)
- Education and past jobs (making sure you didn't lie on your resume)
- Credit report (for jobs in finance or positions of trust)

If you're applying for a job, your employment background report is like your professional autobiography. You want it to be a bestseller, not a cautionary tale.

Insurance Scores: The Crystal Ball of Risk Assessment

Insurance companies use your history to predict how likely you are to cost them money. They look at:

- Claims history (how often you've needed their help)
- Credit information (because apparently, people who pay bills on time are safer drivers)
- Driving record (for car insurance)
- Property history (for home insurance)

Think of insurance scores as a "*safety rating*" for your wallet. The safer you appear, the less you pay. It's like being rewarded for being boring in the best possible way.

Why All This Matters: The Real-Life Impact (AKA Why You Should Care)

These reports aren't just boring paperwork collecting digital dust somewhere. They affect your life in very real, very expensive ways:

Bad credit report consequences:

- Higher interest rates on everything (you pay more just because they don't trust you)
- Getting denied for loans or credit cards
- Landlords rejecting your rental applications
- Some employers passing you over for jobs
- Bad LexisNexis report consequences:
- Difficulty renting apartments
- Higher insurance rates
- Problems getting certain types of loans
- Bad ChexSystems report consequences:
- Banks refusing to let you open checking accounts
- Being forced to use expensive prepaid cards
- Difficulty getting loans or credit

The bottom line: If your reports are messy, companies charge you more or say "*no thanks.*" If your reports are clean, doors open, red carpets roll out, and life gets easier.

Real-world example:
The True Cost of "Buy Now, Pay Later"

Picture this: You buy a $2,000 leather sofa with a store financing offer. With good credit, you qualify for 0% interest; pay it off in 12 months, and it costs you exactly $2,000. But with poor credit, you might get stuck with a 25% APR. If you stretch payments over three years, that same sofa could end up costing you $2,800. That extra $800 isn't just interest, it's the equivalent of:

- A high-end coffee maker you'll never buy,
- A month's worth of groceries,
- Or a weekend getaway you now can't afford.

The kicker? After three years, you're left with the same worn-in couch, just $800 poorer. Financing feels painless in the moment, but debt always collects its price.

How to Check Your Consumer Reports: Become Your Own Financial Detective

Here is the good news: You have the legal right to see these reports. It's like having backstage passes to your own financial show.

Credit Reports:

- Free once a year from all three bureaus at AnnualCreditReport.com
- This is the only official free site, don't be fooled by imposters!
- You can stagger each provider throughout the year (check one every four months)
- LexisNexis Report:
- Request a free copy at consumer.risk.lexisnexis.com
- They're required to give you one free report per year
- ChexSystems Report:
- Free yearly at chexsystems.com
- Essential if you've had banking problems in the past
- Employment Screening Reports:
- Employers must tell you if they use one and get your permission
- You can request a copy from the screening company

Pro tip: Set a calendar reminder to check these reports regularly. It's like going to the dentist; not fun, but necessary for your health (in this case, your financial health).

Fixing Mistakes: Your Superhero Moment

Found a mistake? Don't just shrug and move on, fight for your financial reputation! You have rights under the Fair Credit Reporting Act (FCRA), and you should use them.

Here's your action plan:

1. Contact the company that issued the report
2. File a dispute explaining the mistake in detail
3. Provide documentation if you have it
4. Follow up if you don't hear back within 30 days

They are legally required to investigate and correct errors within 30 days. It's like being a superhero defending your good name, except instead of a cape, you have strongly worded letters and legal rights.

A Quick Story to Drive the Point Home

My friend Mike once got denied for a mortgage even though he had excellent credit and a great job. The problem? His LexisNexis report showed he had been evicted from an apartment for non-payment of rent.

Plot twist: Mike had never even lived at that address. Someone with a similar name had been evicted, and the information got mixed up in the system. It took Mike three months of fighting with LexisNexis to get the mistake corrected, and he almost lost his dream house because of it. The lesson? Don't assume these reports are accurate just because they're "*official.*"

Bottom Line: Know Your Reports, Control Your Destiny

- Here is what you need to remember:
- Your credit report is your debt history and payment behavior.
- Consumer reports are any records companies use to judge you financially.
- Knowledge is power—if you don't know what they're saying about you, you can't defend yourself.
- Mistakes happen—check your reports regularly and dispute errors immediately.
- Your financial reputation affects everything from where you can live to what you pay for insurance.

Think of managing your consumer reports like maintaining your car, regular check-ups prevent major problems down the road.

Your Money Reputation Workout Plan

- ✓ Check your credit report annually (set a calendar reminder)
- ✓ Order other consumer reports (LexisNexis, ChexSystems) yearly
- ✓ Review everything carefully (mistakes are more common than you think)

- ✓ Dispute mistakes immediately (don't wait—errors don't age like wine)
- ✓ Keep accounts in good standing (pay on time, every time)
- ✓ Monitor your reports (some services offer free monitoring)

Think of it like going to the gym for your finances; regular exercise keeps your money reputation in fighting shape!

Why did the credit report go to therapy? Because it had too many issues to work through! But seriously, take care of your reports, and your money life will thank you. Your future self is counting on you to be the responsible, report-checking adult they need you to be. Don't let them down!

Chapter 3: Personal Insurance — How Not to Lose Everything

"Insurance is like an umbrella. You don't need it every day, but when it rains, you'll be glad you have it."

Why Even Bother with Insurance? (AKA Why You Can't Just Wing It)

Picture this: You're 23, fresh out of college, finally making real money, and adulting like a boss. You've got your own place, a decent car, and for the first time in your life, your bank account doesn't make you cry. Then life decides to play a cruel joke.

Maybe it's a fender-bender with a Mercedes (because of course it's a Mercedes). Maybe it's a midnight trip to the ER because that "*weird chest pain*" turned out to be more serious than you thought. Or maybe it's your upstairs neighbor's washing machine exploding like a domestic waterfall, flooding your apartment and turning your *PlayStation* into modern art.

Starting out in adult life can feel like you've been dropped into a video game where nobody explained the rules, and insurance might sound like one of those annoying optional add-ons you skip to save money. You might be thinking:

"I'm healthy as a horse. I've never crashed my car. My apartment is basically a fortress. Why should I spend money on something I'll never use?"

Here is the brutal truth about life: bad things don't check your calendar before showing up uninvited. Accidents, illnesses, and disasters are like that friend who shows up at your door at 2 AM without calling first; inconvenient, unexpected, and potentially very expensive.

One medical emergency, one car crash, or one kitchen fire could wipe out years of your savings faster than you can say "*Well, that escalated quickly.*" We're talking about going from financial stability to financial disaster in the time it takes to order a pizza.

Insurance is like paying a small monthly fee to avoid a disaster-sized bill later. Think of it as hiring a financial bodyguard who's got your back when life decides to throw haymakers at your wallet.

The Big Idea: What Is Insurance, Really?

Insurance is risk management, a fancy phrase that basically means you're paying someone else to share your risk instead of facing it alone like some kind of financial superhero. You're not paying to avoid risk completely (because that's impossible unless you plan to live in a bubble), but you're paying to avoid being financially crushed by it all by yourself.

Here is the simplest way to think about it: Imagine you and 999 other people each put $10 into a big pot every month. That's $10,000 total. Now, if one person in your group gets hit with a $10,000 medical bill, the pot pays for it, and everyone else just keeps contributing their $10. But if YOU'RE the one who gets hit with that bill and you don't have insurance, congratulations; you're on your own with a $10,000 problem. It's like having 999 financial friends who've got your back, and you've got theirs.

Types of Personal Insurance You Actually Need to Know About

Let's break down the most common types of personal insurance in plain English, with real stories and the occasional dad joke because learning about insurance doesn't have to feel like watching paint dry in slow motion.

1. Life Insurance
2. Health Insurance
3. Disability Insurance
4. Auto Insurance
5. Renters Insurance

6. Homeowners Insurance
7. Liability Insurance

1. Life Insurance: Your Financial Hug from Beyond

Life insurance pays money to your family or loved ones you pass away. It's not always needed like when you're young and single (unless you want to implement an early strategy), but if you have kids or someone depends on your income, it can be essential.

There are two main types:

- Term life insurance: Covers you for a specific period (like 10 or 20 years), usually cheaper
- Whole life insurance: Covers you forever and builds cash value, usually more expensive

It's like leaving a financial hug for your family when you're not there to provide for them anymore. Morbid? Maybe. Responsible? Absolutely.

2. Health Insurance: Your Medical Safety Net

This is the big kahuna, the MVP of insurance, the Beyoncé of coverage. Health insurance helps pay for doctor visits, hospital stays, surgeries, prescriptions, and basically anything that happens when your body decides to malfunction. Without health insurance, even a simple broken leg could cost you more than a luxury car. We're talking \$15,000-\$30,000 for surgery, hospital stays, and recovery. For a broken leg! Your leg isn't even made of gold!

Story time:

My friend Dan went to the ER once without insurance because he thought he was having a heart attack during a Netflix binge. Turns out it was just anxiety from realizing he'd been watching *The Office* for 14 hours straight (we've all been there). The bill? \$12,000! He called it his "*surprise car loan*" because who expects a hospital bill to feel like financing a Honda Civic? Dan now has health insurance and has switched to comedy shows only. Even basic health insurance plans can help you avoid financial ruin when life throws you a medical curveball. And trust me, life has a really good pitching arm and terrible aim.

What health insurance typically covers:

- Doctor visits and checkups (including that weird rash you're too embarrassed to Google)
- Emergency room visits (for actual emergencies, not WebMD-induced panic)
- Prescription medications (because generic ibuprofen hits different when insurance pays)
- Surgery and hospital stays (the expensive stuff)
- Preventive care (the stuff that keeps you healthy and saves money long-term)

Pro tip: Even if you're young and healthy, get health insurance. Young people aren't immortal, they just think they are. Your 25-year-old invincibility complex won't negotiate with medical bills.

3. Disability Insurance: Your Paycheck's Backup Plan

This one is often overlooked, but it's super important. If you get sick or injured and can't work, disability insurance pays you a portion of your income. It's like having a financial stunt double for your earning ability. Here is a sobering fact: you're more likely to become disabled during your working years than you are to die. Your ability to work and earn money is probably your biggest asset; protect it like your phone screen!

Types of disability insurance:

- Short-term disability: Provides an income for a few months to a year
- Long-term disability: Provides an income for several years or until retirement

Real-world example:

A friend of mine fell off a ladder while changing a light bulb (yes, really) and broke his back. He couldn't work for eight months. Without disability insurance, he would have lost his house. With it, he got 60% of his salary and could focus on recovery instead of asking AI how to file a bankruptcy. Also, He now pays other people to change his light bulbs.

4. Auto Insurance: Because Cars Don't Fix Themselves

Did you know? In most states, having auto insurance isn't just a good idea, it's the law! Driving without insurance is like playing Russian roulette with your financial future, except every chamber is loaded. Auto insurance usually provides coverage for damage to your car, damage to other people's cars, and injuries to you or others. It's basically your "*oops, I messed up*" protection plan for when physics reminds you who's the boss.

In simple words, what auto insurance typically covers?

- Liability coverage: Provides coverage for the damages or injuries you cause to others (bodily injuries or property damage). It can be required by law.
- Collision coverage: Provides coverage for damage to your car resulting from a collision with another vehicle or object.
- Comprehensive coverage: Provides coverage for damage to your car from non-collision events such as theft, vandalism, hail, or animals.
- Medical payments: Provides coverage for medical expenses for you and your passengers in the event of an accident.

Take your time to talk to your insurance agent and discuss these and all other coverages and endorsements that might be important to you. Of course, as with every insurance policy, read the coverage, limits, and exclusions carefully to understand what is covered and what is not.

Real-world example:

My neighbor Sarah was backing out of a parking spot while checking her phone and backed into a Tesla. (don't @ her, she knows) The repair bill? $8,000. For a bumper! A Tesla bumper costs more than some people's entire cars. Thank goodness for auto insurance, or Sarah would still be eating ramen noodles and crying into her steering wheel.

Pro tip: Don't just get the minimum liability coverage. Accidents can get expensive fast, and you don't want to be the person explaining to a judge why you can't pay for the Ferrari you accidentally rear-ended at a red light.

5. Renters Insurance: Your Stuff's Bodyguard

You might be renting an apartment, a room, or even living in your parents' basement (no judgment here, we've all been there). Renters insurance might cover some of your belongings—your phone, laptop, clothes, that ugly coffee mug you don't want to lose, and your gaming setup—if they get stolen or damaged by fire, theft, or other disasters. It also offers Liability coverage. Again, read the coverage, limits, and exclusions carefully to understand what is covered and what is not.

It's usually incredibly cheap. Sometimes even less than what you probably spend on a single DoorDash order! Plus, it protects you if you accidentally damage your landlord's property. So, when your attempt at making a romantic dinner turns your kitchen into a scene from a disaster movie, renters insurance has your back.

What renters insurance typically covers:

- Your personal belongings (yes, even those weird vintage band t-shirts)
- Temporary living expenses if your place becomes unlivable
- Liability if someone gets hurt in your apartment
- Story time:

My friend Marcus's apartment got broken into while he was at work. The thieves took his laptop, TV, gaming console, AirPods, and even his good silverware (who steals silverware?! Apparently, criminals with refined taste). Without renters insurance, he would have been out about $4,000. With it? He paid a $250 deductible and got money to replace his stuff. He even upgraded his TV and called it his "*crime dividend*."

6. Homeowners Insurance: Your Castle's Shield

When you borrow money to buy a house, homeowners' insurance is usually required by your lender. It protects the building, your belongings, and you if someone gets hurt on your property. It's like having a bouncer for your house, except instead of keeping out drunk people, it keeps out financial disasters.

What homeowners' insurance typically covers:

- The structure of your home (walls, roof, foundation—the important stuff)
- Your personal belongings (inside and outside of your property)
- Liability if someone gets injured on your property
- Additional living expenses if your home becomes temporarily unlivable

Think of it as a comprehensive shield for your castle, protecting you from financial dragons that might try to burn down your savings.

7. Liability Insurance: Your "Please Don't Sue Me" Protection

Ever worried about getting sued? In America, people sue each other more often than they change their Netflix passwords. Liability insurance protects you if someone sues you for injury or damages. It's often included in renters or homeowners' insurance, but you can also buy extra coverage called "umbrella insurance" for additional protection.

When you might need liability insurance:

- Someone slips and falls at your place
- You accidentally cause a car accident

- Your dog bites someone (even if your dog is usually an angel)
- You accidentally damage someone else's property

Prioritizing Financial Risks

Financial experts often recommend that you cover risks starting from the most catastrophic to the least catastrophic. From my perspective, losing the breadwinner of the family is one of the most devastating events that can occur. Imagine not only dealing with the emotional pain of losing a loved one but also suddenly losing the income that the family depends on to pay bills, put food on the table, and plan for the future.

When you think about it, the numbers tell a powerful story: if the primary earner's income disappears forever, it can create financial hardship that lasts for years. That's why life insurance isn't just about money—it's about protecting your family's security when they need it most.

Do the math, and you'll see why covering this risk should be a top priority in your financial strategy.

Priority order:

1. Life insurance (if people depend on your income)
2. Health insurance (non-negotiable, like oxygen)
3. Disability insurance (You cannot work but still alive spending)

4. Auto insurance (if you drive)
5. Renters or homeowners' insurance
6. Liability insurance

Think of it like ordering at a restaurant; get the essentials first, then add the extras if you can afford them.

Why Is Insurance So Important? (Besides the Obvious)

Bad luck is like gravity, it affects everyone equally, regardless of how careful you are. Insurance keeps you from losing all your savings and going into debt when life decides to test your financial stability. Without insurance, you could end up owing more money than you'll earn in years. We're talking about a financial hole so deep you'd need a ladder to see rock bottom. Imagine life is a game of Jenga. Insurance is the steady hand that helps keep your financial tower from crashing when life inevitably removes one of your pieces. And trust me, life loves playing Jenga with your finances.

How Much Insurance Do You Need? (The Goldilocks Principle)

There is no one-size-fits-all answer, but here's a good rule of thumb: Get enough insurance to protect what you can't afford to lose. You don't need the fanciest, most expensive policy with every bell and whistle, just coverage that protects what matters most to your financial stability.

Life Insurance Tip: How Much Do You Really Need?

Figuring out how much life insurance to get can feel tricky, but here's an easy way to start: multiply your annual income by ten. That's it! This simple "rule of thumb" is a great starting point because, honestly, something is better than nothing when it comes to protecting your loved ones.

Of course, there are more detailed ways to calculate the perfect amount—using scientific methods and factoring in your unique financial situation. But if you're just getting started, this quick calculation gives you a solid ballpark figure.

Bonus Tip: Don't rely only on life insurance through your job. Employer-provided life insurance is a nice bonus, but it usually offers much less coverage than you actually need. Plus, if you change jobs, you typically lose that coverage and getting new life insurance later might be harder or more expensive.

So, think of employer life insurance as a little extra, but consider getting your own policy outside of work to make sure your family stays protected no matter what.

Don't Be This Guy: A Cautionary Tale

Meet Joe. Joe was convinced he didn't need insurance because he was "*careful and smart.*" Joe said things like:

"I don't need insurance. I'm a good driver!"
"I never get sick. I eat organic!"
"Nothing bad ever happens to me!"

Then life happened:

- Someone ran a red light and totaled his car ($15,000 in damages)
- He slipped on ice, broke his leg, and owed ($18,000 in medical bills)
- His apartment caught fire, and he lost everything ($25,000 in belongings)

Joe learned the hard way that insurance isn't about betting you'll mess up, it's about protecting yourself when life messes with you. Don't be Joe. Joe is now eating ramen noodles and living in his parents' basement at age 30, not by choice. Joe has become a cautionary tale that insurance agents tell their kids at bedtime.

How to Shop for Insurance (Without Getting Scammed)

Shopping for insurance is like dating, you don't marry the first person you meet, and you definitely don't choose based on looks alone.

Here's your insurance shopping strategy:

1. Understand what's covered—and what's not (read the fine print, even if it's boring)
2. Don't just pick the cheapest policy (sometimes you get what you pay for)

3. Consider the deductible (how much you pay before insurance kicks in)
4. Check the company's reputation (reviews, ratings, how they handle claims)
5. Look for the financial strength of the insurer (Fortune ranking, financial stability, and longevity)—this ensures the company can pay claims now and in the future
6. Know your agent (education, credentials, integrity, professionalism)—a trustworthy and knowledgeable agent can help you navigate your options
7. Review your coverage annually (your needs change, and so should your insurance)

Pro tip: Ask questions until you understand your policies. Insurance agents are paid to explain things to you, so make them earn their money. Don't nod and smile if you're confused, your future self will thank you for being "annoying" now.

Real-World Insurance Costs (So You Can Budget)

Here are some hypothetical examples to help a young adult start an initial budget. Be sure to replace these numbers with actual quotes provided by a licensed insurance agent of a reputable insurer when applying them:

- Health insurance: $150-$400+ per month (depending on your plan and location)

- Auto insurance: $100-$300 per month (depending on your car, location, and driving record)
- Renters insurance: $10-$30 per month
- Life insurance: $20-$50 per month for basic term coverage
- Disability insurance: $50-$150 per month

Remember: these are rough estimates. Your actual costs will depend on your specific situation, location, and coverage needs. Also, these numbers might change faster than TikTok trends, so always get current quotes.

The Bottom Line: Insurance Math

Insurance doesn't make you rich, but it keeps you from going broke. It's part of being a responsible adult who's ready to face life's surprises without having a financial panic attack. Think of it this way: Would you rather pay $200 a month for insurance or $20,000 all at once when disaster strikes? The math is pretty simple, even for people who failed calculus.

Your Insurance Action Plan

✓ Always have health insurance (even if it's just catastrophic coverage)

✓ Don't drive without auto insurance (it's literally illegal in most places)

- ✓ Protect your stuff with renters or homeowners insurance (thing happens)
- ✓ Review your coverage every year (life changes, and so should your insurance)
- ✓ Ask questions until you understand your policies (ignorance isn't bliss when it comes to insurance)
- ✓ Keep your insurance cards in your wallet (you never know when you'll need them)

Final Thought

"Insurance is the safety net under your financial life. Don't walk the tightrope without it."

Remember: You're not paying for insurance hoping you'll need it, you're paying for it hoping you'll never need it. But if you do need it, you'll be really glad you have it. It's like wearing a seatbelt, you don't plan on crashing, but you're sure happy it's there when physics gets involved.

Let's End with a Little Laugh

Why don't insurance agents ever play hide and seek? Because good luck hiding when they're always finding risks! *(But seriously, those risks are real, and insurance helps you manage them. Your future self will thank you for being responsible today. Also, your future self will probably have better taste in jokes.)*

Chapter 4: Savings — Your Modern Piggy Bank

"Saving money isn't about being rich. It's about not being broke when life surprises you."

Why Save? (Or: How to Not Panic When Life Gets Expensive)

Picture this: You just got your first real paycheck after college. You're staring at that direct deposit notification like it's a love letter, thinking, "*Finally! I can buy what I want!*" Maybe it's that new phone case that costs more than your entire high school wardrobe, those sneakers you've been stalking on Instagram, or that extra-large pizza with every topping known to humanity (including the weird ones).

You feel rich. You feel powerful. You feel like you could buy a small country (or at least a really nice coffee maker). But here's the reality check that hits harder than your college alarm clock:

Emergencies don't care about your shopping list. Bills don't wait for payday. Your car doesn't break down when it's convenient. Your laptop doesn't die right after you get paid, it dies the day before rent is due, because technology has a twisted sense of humor.

Opportunities often knock when you're ready for them. That dream job might require you to move across the country. Your friend might invite you on a last-minute trip to Europe. Your roommate might move out suddenly, leaving you with double rent until you find a replacement.

Saving money gives you freedom and security. It's like having a secret weapon for life's unexpected battles, except instead of a sword, it's a bank account that doesn't judge you for eating cereal for dinner three nights in a row.

The Big Idea: What Is Saving?

Saving is like paying yourself first, but cooler. Imagine you have two roommates living in your head named Present You and Future You.

Present You is like that friend who always wants to order takeout, buy unnecessary gadgets, and live like money grows on trees. Present You says things like, "YOLO!" and "*I'll worry about tomorrow tomorrow.*"

Future You is the responsible one who wants to have some cash saved for rainy days, emergencies, and that inevitable moment when your phone screen cracks and you need $200 to fix it (again).

Saving means choosing Future You over Present You's immediate cravings. It's your financial safety cushion, your modern piggy bank that keeps you from having financial meltdowns in Target when your card gets declined.

Think of it this way: saving is like having a financial superhero cape. You might not need it every day, but when life throws a villain your way, you'll be ready to fly instead of falling flat on your face.

What's an Emergency Fund? (AKA Your "Oh Crap" Money)

An emergency fund is money you don't touch except for real emergencies. Think of it as your "*break glass in case of emergency*" fund, except the glass is your willpower and the emergency is your car making that weird noise that definitely wasn't there yesterday.

Use it for:

- ✓ Car breaks down (and starts making sounds like a dying robot)
- ✓ Medical bills (because apparently being healthy is expensive)
- ✓ Job loss (when your boss decides to "restructure" you out of employment)

- ✓ Unexpected travel (family emergency, not a spontaneous Vegas trip)
- ✓ Major appliance failure (when your washing machine decides to flood your apartment)

Don't use it for:

- ✗ New shoes (no matter how cute they are or how much they're "on sale")
- ✗ Concert tickets (even if it's your favorite artist and you'll "literally die" if you miss it)
- ✗ Takeout because you're too lazy to cook (we've all been there, but that's not an emergency)
- ✗ That "limited edition" anything that will definitely be worth millions someday
- ✗ Retail therapy after a bad day (your bank account needs therapy too)

Real talk:

The hardest part about emergency funds isn't saving the money, it's not spending it on things that feel like emergencies but aren't. That flash sale on your favorite store? Not an emergency. Your friend's birthday dinner at that expensive restaurant? Not an emergency. Running out of your favorite snacks? Definitely not an emergency (despite what your brain might tell you at 2 AM).

How Much Should I Save? (The Magic Numbers)

The gold standard is 3 to 6 months of living expenses saved up. But don't let that number scare you into not starting! That's like saying you need to run a marathon before you can jog around the block.

Start with baby steps:

- First goal: $500 (That's like a superhero shield for small emergencies)
- Then aim for: $1,000 (Now you're getting serious)
- Keep building from there: Work toward that 3-6 month goal

Here's some perspective: If your monthly expenses are $2,000, then 3-6 months would be $6,000-$12,000. Sounds impossible? It's not. It's just a marathon, not a sprint.

Pro tip: Don't get overwhelmed by the big number. Even $500 can save you from a lot of financial stress. It's the difference between a minor inconvenience and a major crisis.

Where to Keep It? (Location, Location, Location)

Keep your emergency fund in a savings account; easy enough to access when needed, but not so easy that you spend it on a midnight Amazon shopping spree.

Here's the strategy:

- Keep it separate from your checking account to avoid temptation (out of sight, out of mind)
- Consider a high-yield savings account if you want your money to grow a little with interest (it's like getting paid to save)
- Don't invest it in stocks or cryptocurrency; emergency funds should be boring and predictable, not exciting and volatile

Why not under your mattress? Because your mattress doesn't pay interest, and also because that's weird. This isn't a movie from the 1920s.

Why not in your checking account? Because checking accounts are like having cookies on your counter; too tempting and too easy to access when you're feeling financially hungry.

Why Not Just Use Credit? (The Debt Trap Explained)

Here's a simple rule that will save you from a lot of financial pain: **Credit is for borrowing. Savings is for surviving.**

Credit means debt you have to repay, usually with interest that makes loan sharks look generous. Savings is your own money, no strings attached, no monthly payments, no guilt. When an emergency hits, you want cash ready; not a loan application and three business days of waiting while your car sits broken in a parking lot.

Credit card interest rates can be 20-30% annually.

That means if you put a $1,000 emergency on a credit card and only make minimum payments, you could end up paying $1,500 or more by the time it's paid off. That's like buying the same emergency twice.

Savings account interest might be 1-5% annually.

Your $1,000 emergency fund might earn you $10-50 per year. Not life-changing, but at least it's growing instead of shrinking.

Don't Be This Guy: A Cautionary Tale

My friend Alex had no emergency fund because he was "*living his best life*" (translation: spending every penny on experiences and avocado toast). His car broke down on a Tuesday. The repair bill was $800. He put it on a credit card with 25% interest, thinking he'd pay it off quickly. But then his laptop died. Then his phone screen cracked. Then his cat got sick (apparently pets don't care about your budget either).

Six months later, he was paying minimum payments on $3,000 of debt and still didn't have an emergency fund. The interest alone was costing him $60 per month. He was literally paying $60 monthly for the privilege of having had emergencies.

Plot twist: He sold that car a year later and bought a different one. But he was still paying for the old car's repairs on his credit card. Don't be Alex. Be the person with the secret stash of savings who sleeps peacefully at night.

How to Start Saving (The Practical Magic)

Step 1: Automate It (Set It and Forget It)

Set up automatic transfers on payday. Pay yourself before you spend. Most banks let you set up automatic transfers from checking to savings. It's like having a responsible financial assistant who never takes a day off.

Start small: Even $25 per paycheck adds up. That's $650 per year if you're paid bi-weekly. Not bad for money you won't even miss.

Step 2: Start Small (Baby Steps Count)

$10 a week adds up faster than you think. Don't wait until you "*have extra*" money, you never will! Extra money is like unicorns: everyone talks about them, but no one actually sees them.

Math time: $10 per week = $520 per year. $20 per week = $1,040 per year. See? You're already building that emergency fund.

Step 3: Cut Unnecessary Expenses (The Subscription Audit)

Cancel subscriptions you don't use. You know, that streaming service you signed up for to watch one show and forgot about, or that gym membership you've been "*meaning to use.*"

The latte factor: Making coffee at home instead of buying it can save you $5-10 per day. That's $1,825-$3,650 per year. Suddenly that emergency fund doesn't seem so impossible.

Cook at home: Meal planning isn't just for fitness influencers. It's for people who want to save money and eat better. That $15 lunch can become a $3 homemade meal.

Step 4: Find Extra Money (The Treasure Hunt)

- Sell stuff you don't need (that exercise bike collecting dust might fund your emergency fund)
- Pick up a side hustle (freelance work, pet sitting, selling crafts)
- Use cash back apps and credit card rewards (if you pay them off monthly)
- Put tax refunds, bonuses, and gift money directly into savings

Pro Tip: The Invisible Money Trick

"Make savings invisible. If you don't see it, you won't spend it."

This is the best money advice you'll ever get. When your savings automatically disappears from your checking account, you'll adjust your spending to what's left. It's like magic, but with more financial responsibility.

Advanced level: Set up your direct deposit to automatically split between checking and savings. You'll never even see the money you're saving, so you won't miss it.

The Emotional Side of Saving (It's Not Just About Numbers)

Saving money isn't just about spreadsheets and bank balances. It's about peace of mind, confidence, and sleeping better at night.

Financial stress is real stress. When you're worried about money, everything else feels harder. Work is more stressful. Relationships are more tense. Even fun activities feel less fun when you're worried about affording them.

Savings = freedom. When you have money saved, you can:

- Say no to things you hate
- Help friends and family when they need it
- Take advantage of opportunities
- Handle problems without panic
- Sleep like a baby (a very financially responsible baby)

Think of it like this: *"Money in the bank is sleep at night."* When you have savings, you can breathe easier, sleep better, and face the day like a financial ninja. You're not just surviving, you're thriving.

The Psychology of Saving (Why It's Hard and How to Make It Easier)

Why saving feels impossible:

- Our brains are wired for instant gratification
- We underestimate future needs and overestimate present wants
- We think we'll be more disciplined "next month"
- We compare ourselves to others who seem to have it all figured out

How to hack your brain:

- Automate everything (remove the decision from your daily life)
- Set up visual reminders (chart your progress, celebrate milestones)
- Make it a game (challenge yourself to save a certain amount each month)
- Find a savings buddy (accountability partners work for money too)
- Focus on the feeling (imagine how good it will feel to handle an emergency without stress)

Bottom Line: Your Financial Safety Net

Emergencies will happen. It's not a matter of if, it's a matter of when. Your phone will break. Your car will need repairs. Your laptop will die at the worst possible moment. Your pet will get sick. You might lose a job or need to move unexpectedly. Savings turns these situations from a crisis into just an inconvenience. Instead of panicking, you'll think, "*Well, this sucks, but at least I can handle it.*"

Start now. Build your cushion. Your future self will thank you, probably while sitting in a comfortable chair instead of crying in a parking lot.

Your Savings Action Plan

- ✓ Open a savings account just for emergencies (separate from your checking)
- ✓ Automate transfers every payday (start with whatever you can afford)
- ✓ Don't touch it unless it's a real emergency (be honest with yourself)
- ✓ Increase your savings as you earn more (lifestyle inflation is real, but so is savings inflation)
- ✓ Review and adjust regularly (life changes, and so should your savings goals)

✓ Celebrate milestones (reaching $500, $1,000, or your first full month of expenses is a big deal)

Final Thought

"Saving isn't punishment. It's self-respect for your future."

Every dollar you save is a vote of confidence in your future self. You're saying, "*I believe in you, and I want to make sure you're prepared for whatever comes next.*" It's not about being cheap or missing out on fun. It's about being smart and prepared. It's about turning from someone who worries about money into someone who has money handle the worrying.

Let's End with a Little Laugh

Why did the piggy bank break up with the wallet? Because it needed some space to grow! *(But seriously, give your savings some space to grow. Compound interest is earning interest over interest and might be small now, but it's like a financial strategy that grows slowly and then all at once. Your future self will be amazed by what a little consistent saving can accomplish.)*

Chapter 5: Checking Accounts and Tracking Your Expenses

"Your checking account isn't a magic wallet. If you don't track it, it disappears."

Why Have a Checking Account? (AKA Your Financial Home Base)

Picture this: You just landed your first real job in the USA, congratulations! You're feeling like a responsible adult, maybe even considering buying groceries instead of living off ramen and hope. Then your boss asks, "*Where should we direct-deposit your pay?*"

You might think, "*Uh, I don't know... under my mattress? In a shoebox? Can you just Venmo me?*"

Nope! That's where a checking account comes in. It's like your money's home base, your personal cash headquarters, your financial command center where all the magic happens.

Your checking account is your main hub for:

- Getting paid (because mattresses don't accept direct deposits)
- Paying bills (utilities, rent, that subscription you forgot you had)
- Buying things with your debit card (groceries, gas, questionable 2 AM online purchases)
- Sending money to friends (or paying back that pizza debt you've been avoiding)

Without a checking account, you'd be stuck carrying cash around like it's 1985, or worse, going to those expensive check-cashing places that charge you money just to access your own money. It's like paying a toll to enter your own house. And we all know cash has a mysterious ability to disappear faster than snacks at a college dorm party. One minute you have $60, the next minute you're digging through couch cushions looking for enough quarters to buy a coffee.

The Big Idea: What Is a Checking Account?

Think of a checking account as your daily money home. It's not where your money goes to retire (that's savings), but where it hangs out while waiting for instructions. It keeps your cash safe from pirates (or your own impulse purchases), helps you pay bills easily, and leaves a clear digital trail of your spending so you don't accidentally buy 10 pizzas in one week.

Actually, let's be honest; if you're tracking your expenses properly, you might discover you *are* buying 10 pizzas in one week, and that's valuable information about your life choices.

How Does It Work? (The Simple Version)

It's beautifully simple:

1. You deposit money (paychecks, transfers from friends or family, birthday money from grandma)
2. You withdraw money (using an ATM, debit card, writing checks, or online payments)
3. The bank tracks it all for you (like a very organized, very boring personal assistant)

Imagine it as your money's inbox and outbox. Money comes in, money goes out, and your bank keeps score like a financial referee. The best part? Unlike your brain, the bank remembers everything.

The Danger of Not Tracking (AKA The $50 Pizza Story)

Here is the brutal truth: Your debit card is NOT bottomless, despite what your 2 AM brain might tell you when you're ordering takeout.

If you don't pay attention:

- Your account can go negative, and suddenly your bank becomes your worst frenemy

- You might spend more than you have (shocking, I know)
- The bank processes the transaction and then charges you an overdraft fee. This fee will sneak up on you like a financial ninja (sometimes $35 or more per transaction!)

A Real-Life Horror Story:

My friend Dan didn't check his balance one weekend. He was out with friends, feeling generous, and bought a pizza for $15. Plot twist: he only had $10 left in his account. The bank charged him a $35 overdraft fee. That pizza? Suddenly a $50 pizza! He still talks about it as "*the most expensive pizza of my life,*" and it wasn't even that good.

Moral of the story: Always check your balance before ordering extra cheese. Your future self will thank you, and your wallet will stop crying.

How to Avoid That Disaster (Your Financial Survival Kit)

Here are some easy ways to keep your account in the green and your stress levels in the normal range:

1. **Check Your Balance Often (Like, Really Often)**: Make it a habit. Check it when you wake up, check it before you spend, check it before you sleep. It should

become as automatic as checking your phone for notifications.

2. **Use Your Bank's App (Your Pocket Financial Spy)**: Most banks have apps that are actually pretty decent. Download it. Love it. Let it become your financial best friend. It's like having a tiny accountant in your pocket, except it doesn't judge you for buying coffee every day.
3. **Set Up Alerts for Low Balance**: Your phone will yell at you when you're running low. It's like having a financial smoke detector; annoying when it goes on, but you'll be grateful it's there.
4. **Write Down Big Expenses**: Don't trust your memory. Your brain is great at many things, but remembering that you spent $80 on groceries yesterday is not one of them. Write it down, put it in your phone, tattoo it on your arm; whatever works.
5. **Don't Count Pending Deposits Before They Clear**: Waiting is hard, but your bank needs time to process deposits. That paycheck might show as "*pending*" for a day or two. Don't spend it until it's actually, officially, really-truly-no-takebacks in your account.

Using Your Debit Card (The Magic Money Door)

Your debit card is linked directly to your checking account. It's safer than carrying cash around (no more sweaty palms at the bus stop, no more panic when you can't find your wallet). But remember: spending is instant. Swipe and your money leaves immediately.

Think of it like a magic door, once you open it, the money rushes out! There's no "*oops, I changed my mind*" button. It's gone faster than your motivation to go to the gym.

Pro tip: Some people find it helpful to use cash for discretionary spending (coffee, entertainment, impulse purchases) because it makes spending feel more real. When you hand over actual paper money, your brain registers it differently than swiping a card.

Bills and Online Payments (The Adulting Automation)

Most bills these days can be paid automatically. Rent, utilities, phone bills, streaming services, gym memberships you forgot you had, you name it. Setting up automatic payments can save you from late fees and awkward phone calls from your landlord at 8 AM. But be careful: make sure you have enough money in your account, or your payments might bounce like a rubber ball, and then you're stuck with late fees AND angry phone calls. It's like setting up dominos; one falls, and suddenly everything is chaos.

Strategy: Set up automatic payments for fixed bills (rent, utilities, insurance), but pay variable expenses (groceries, gas, entertainment) manually so you stay aware of your spending.

Checks? What Are Those? (The Dinosaur Payment Method)

Checks might seem old-fashioned, like flip phones or people who still use Facebook, but some landlords and companies still use them. It's like they're stuck in a time warp where everything was slower and required more paperwork. However, checks are still in use and you may need to use them occasionally.

If you write a check, make sure you have the funds. A bounced check is like a financial boomerang; you throw it, and it hits you right back with fees and angry landlords. Plus, it's embarrassing. Nobody wants to be the person whose check bounced.

Fun fact: Many young adults have never written a check. If you're one of them, ask someone to show you how, or watch a YouTube tutorial. It's a life skill you hope you'll never need, but inevitably will.

Bank Fees to Watch For (The Sneaky Money Ninjas)

Banks aren't just your friends; sometimes, they're sneaky fee ninjas hiding in the shadows, waiting to strike your account. Watch out for:

Monthly Maintenance Fees

Some banks charge you money just for the privilege of keeping your money there. It's like paying rent to live in your own house. Ask if there's a free account option, there usually is.

Overdraft Fees (The Sneakiest of All)

We've covered these, but they're worth mentioning again. $35 for spending $1 more than you have? That's a quick way to lose your money.

ATM Fees

Using another bank's machine can cost you $3-5 per transaction. That's like paying a toll to access your own money. Plan ahead and use your bank's ATMs, or get cash back at grocery stores.

Paper Statement Fees

Some banks charge for mailing paper statements. Go digital, it's free, and you'll help save trees. Mother Earth will thank you.

How to Choose a Good Checking Account (Your Financial Dating Guide)

Shopping for a checking account is like dating, but with less emotional baggage and more fee schedules. Look for:

No or Low Monthly Fees

Free is better than cheap, and cheap is better than expensive. Some banks offer free accounts if you meet certain requirements (direct deposit, minimum balance, etc.).

Free Online Banking

Go for it! Because who wants to stand in line at a bank branch? This is 2025, not 1925. You should be able to manage your money from your phone while wearing pajamas.

Convenient ATMs

Look for ATMs near your home, work, or favorite hangout spots. Having to drive across town to avoid fees defeats the purpose.

Good Customer Service

Someone who answers the phone! And ideally, someone who speaks your language and doesn't make you feel bad for asking questions.

Mobile App That Actually Works

A clunky app will make you hate banking. Look for apps with good reviews and features you'll actually use.

Pro Tip: The Envelope Method (Digital Edition)

"Treat your checking account like your wallet with receipts. Always know what's in there."

Some people find it helpful to mentally divide their checking account into categories: rent money, food money, fun money, etc. You can even use separate accounts for different purposes, or just keep track in a notebook or app.

Quick Story: The Vanishing Paycheck Mystery

My cousin David got paid on Friday. By Sunday, it was gone. Completely gone. He said, "*I don't even know where it went. It's like it evaporated.*"

The solution? Tracking. He started writing down every expense, no matter how small. Next month, he saved $200 just by realizing how much went to coffee and takeout. Turns out, his wallet was a sneaky little money vacuum, and small purchases were adding up to major expenses.

The math was shocking: $5 coffee × 20 days = $100/month. $12 lunch × 15 days = $180/month. Two restaurant dinners per week = $120/month. That's $400 per month on food alone, not including groceries!

David now makes coffee at home and meal preps. He still goes out, but now it's intentional, not accidental.

The Power of Tracking (Your Financial Superpower)

Tracking your money gives you:

- Awareness = control
- Control = less stress
- Less stress = better decisions

- Better decisions = more money

It's like having a financial GPS instead of wandering in the dark. You'll know exactly where your money is going, and more importantly, you'll know where you want it to go.

The psychology behind it: When you track expenses, you become more mindful of spending. It's like when you start counting calories; suddenly you're aware of every bite. The act of tracking itself changes your behavior.

How to Track Expenses (Choose Your Own Adventure)

Find a method that works for you. The best tracking system is the one you'll actually use.

Option 1: Your Bank App

Many banks have budgeting tools built-in. They automatically categorize your spending, which is like having a financial assistant who never sleeps.

Option 2: Old School Notebook

Write them down in a notebook. It's old school but effective. There's something about physically writing down "$12 for lunch" that makes it feel more real.

Option 3: Budget Apps

Use apps to track expenses or even a simple spreadsheet. Technology can make tracking easier, but don't get so caught up in finding the perfect app that you never start tracking.

Option 4: The Receipt Method

Keep all your receipts for a week and review them. It's like doing a financial autopsy on your spending habits.

Categories to track:

- Housing (rent, utilities)
- Food (groceries, restaurants, coffee)
- Transportation (gas, public transit, rideshares)
- Entertainment (movies, streaming, going out)
- Shopping (clothes, random stuff)
- Miscellaneous (the mysterious "where did this money go?" category)

The Weekly Money Date (Make It a Habit)

Schedule a weekly "*money date*" with yourself. Review your spending, check your account balance, and plan for the week ahead. It sounds boring, but it's like going to the gym for your finances.

Make it fun: Do it at a coffee shop, play your favorite music, reward yourself with something small when you stick to your budget. The goal is to make it a positive experience, not a punishment.

Bottom Line: Your Money, Your Rules

Your checking account is your daily money tool. Don't let it surprise you like a magician's disappearing act. Track it. Respect it. Make it work for you. Think of your checking account as your money's home base. Just like you keep your actual home organized and know where things are, you should keep your financial home organized and know where your money is.

Your Money Management Action Plan

- ✓ Check your balance regularly (make it a daily habit)
- ✓ Review transactions weekly (catch mistakes before they catch you)
- ✓ Set up low-balance alerts (let technology be your safety net)
- ✓ Track spending categories (knowledge is power)
- ✓ Avoid overdrafts like the plague (seriously, those fees are deadly)
- ✓ Automate fixed bills (but stay aware of variable expenses)
- ✓ Choose a bank that works for you (not against you)

Final Thought

"Your money is a tool. Learn to use it, or it will use you."

Your checking account isn't just a place to keep money, it's your financial command center. The better you understand it and manage it, the more control you have over your financial life. And control over your money means control over your stress, your options, and your future.

Let's End with a Little Laugh

Why don't secrets last in a bank? Because the teller always spills the beans! *(But seriously, banks are actually pretty good at keeping secrets. They're just not so good at keeping your money secret from you, which is why tracking is so important. Your money wants to be found, counted, and managed responsibly. Don't disappoint it.)*

Chapter 6: Why Everything Costs More Every Year — Inflation Made Simple

"Inflation is like your money going to the gym in reverse— it gets weaker every year."

The Great Mystery of the Shrinking Dollar

Picture this: You walk into your favorite coffee shop, the same one you've been going to since you started working. You order your usual; a medium coffee, nothing fancy. The barista says, " *That'll be $4.50.*"

Wait, what? Didn't this same coffee cost $3.75 last year? And $3.25 the year before that?

Your brain starts spinning: *"Did they change the recipe? Is this now made with unicorn tears? Did I accidentally order the premium 'liquid gold' version?"*

Nope. Welcome to inflation, the sneaky financial phenomenon that makes your money feel like it's on a diet, getting smaller and weaker every year.

What Is Inflation? (The Simple Truth)

Inflation is basically when stuff gets more expensive over time. Not because the stuff got better, not because you're suddenly shopping at fancy places, but because that's just how money works in the real world. Think of it like this: Your dollar bill is like a superhero, but instead of getting stronger with age, it gets weaker. Every year, it can lift a little less, carry a little less, and buy a little less. Same cape, same costume, but somehow less powerful.

It's not personal, inflation doesn't have it out for you specifically. It's just the economic equivalent of gravity: always there, always working, whether you notice it or not.

The Burger Time Machine Story

Let's take a trip in our imaginary time machine. Ready? *Whoosh!* We're back in 2005. You walk into McDonald's with a crisp $1 bill. You can buy a burger off the dollar menu and feel like a financial genius. Life is good.

Whoosh! Fast forward to 2025. You walk into that same McDonald's with the same $1 bill. The teenage cashier looks at you like you just tried to pay with Monopoly money. That burger? It's now $3.49, and they'll probably ask if you want to add fries and a drink for just $2.99 more.

Your dollar didn't lose its intelligence. The burger didn't get three times more delicious. Inflation happened. It's like your money went to a reverse gym instead of getting stronger, it got weaker, and now it can't lift the same financial weights it used to.

Why Does This Happen? (The Inflation Origin Story)

Inflation happens for a bunch of reasons, but here are the main villains in this financial story:

The Popular Kid Effect: Remember high school? When something became popular, everyone wanted it. Same thing happens with products. When everyone wants the new iPhone, Nintendo Switch, or trendy sneakers, prices go up because demand is high but supply is limited.

The Rising Costs Domino Effect: When it costs more to make stuff; higher wages, more expensive materials, pricier gas for shipping, companies pass those costs to you. It's like when your favorite restaurant has to charge more because rent went up. They're not being mean; they're just trying to stay in business.

The Supply Chain Hiccup: Sometimes factories close, ships get stuck in canals, or natural disasters mess up production. When there's less stuff to go around, prices go up faster than your stress level during finals week.

The "Too Much Money" Problem: When there's a lot of money floating around the economy but not enough products to buy, it's like having too many people at a concert, everyone starts bidding higher for the good seats.

Is Inflation Always the Bad Guy?

Plot twist: A little bit of inflation is actually normal and healthy, like having a small amount of stress that keeps you motivated.

When inflation is low and steady (around 2-3% per year), it usually means:

- The economy is growing
- People are spending money (which keeps businesses happy)
- Wages can grow too (hopefully)

But when inflation goes crazy, like 8%, 10%, or higher, it's like your money is melting like ice cream in July. That's when things get scary.

How Inflation Sneaks Up on You (The Stealth Attack)

Inflation doesn't send you a warning text saying, "*Hey, your money is about to be worth less tomorrow!*" It's sneaky. Here's how it gets you:

Your Everyday Stuff Gets Pricier

- Groceries: That $50 weekly grocery bill becomes $60, then $70

- Gas: Remember when gas was under $2? Pepperidge Farm remembers
- Rent: Your landlord's annual "market adjustment" letter
- Entertainment: Movie tickets, concerts, even streaming services inch up

The Netflix Effect: Remember when Netflix was $7.99? Now it's... well, let's just say it's not $7.99 anymore. And somehow you have three streaming services when you swore you'd only ever need one.

The Mattress Money Disaster Story: My neighbor, let's call him Bob, thought he was a financial genius. In 2010, he saved $5,000 in cash and hid it under his mattress. "*No bank fees, no risk, just safe money,*" he said proudly.

Fast forward to 2025. Bob still has his $5,000. But here's the kicker: what that $5,000 could buy in 2010 would cost about $7,000 today. Bob's money didn't disappear, but its buying power did.

It's like Bob saved 5,000 energy drinks, but inflation turned them into 3,500 energy drinks. Same number of bills, but they just don't go as far. Bob's money was safe from bank failures, market crashes, and fees. But it wasn't safe from inflation; the silent money thief that works 24/7, 365 days a year.

Your Paycheck vs. Inflation: The Endless Race

Imagine you're on a treadmill. Every year, the treadmill gets a little faster (that's inflation), but your running speed (your paycheck) stays the same. You're working just as hard, but you're not moving forward; you're actually falling behind. That is why putting your money to earn interest is smart.

Real talk: If your money grows by 3% but inflation is 5%, your purchasing power actually dropped by 2%. It might look like your savings are increasing, but your wallet knows the truth.

The Debt Plot Twist

Here is where inflation gets interesting. If you have debt with a fixed interest rate (like a car loan or mortgage), inflation can actually be your friend. You're paying back the loan with "*cheaper*" dollars. For example, if you borrowed $10,000 in 2020 and inflation has made everything 20% more expensive, you're essentially paying back the equivalent of $8,000 in 2020 dollars. It's like getting a discount on your debt. But credit cards? They're usually variable interest rates, so they adjust with inflation. They're like that friend who always finds a way to make sure they don't lose money in any situation.

The Ice Cube Analogy (Your Money's Melting Point)

Think of your money as ice cubes at a summer barbecue. Inflation is the heat. If you just leave your ice cubes sitting there, they'll melt away bit by bit. You'll still have water, but it's not as useful as ice. But if you put those ice cubes in a cooler (savings account with interest) or a freezer (investments), they might stay frozen or even multiply into more ice cubes. The goal isn't to stop the heat (you can't control inflation), but to find better ways to protect and grow your ice cubes.

When Inflation Goes Completely Insane

Sometimes inflation loses its mind completely. This is called hyperinflation, and it's like financial horror movie material. Imagine going to buy bread in the morning for $3, and by evening, the same bread costs $6. In some countries, people literally carry wheelbarrows of cash to buy groceries because money becomes nearly worthless. The good news? This is extremely rare in stable countries like the US. Our inflation might be annoying, but it's not "*wheelbarrow of cash*" level crazy.

Your Anti-Inflation Battle Plan

You can't stop inflation (sorry, that's above your pay grade), but you can prepare for it:

1. **Track Your Spending Like a Financial Detective**: Prices change gradually, so you might not notice right away. But if you're tracking your expenses, you'll see when your grocery bill creeps up or when your usual entertainment costs more.
2. **Don't Keep All Your Money in Cash**: This is the hardest lesson for people who grew up thinking cash under the mattress is the safest option. Some cash for emergencies? Absolutely. All your money in cash? That's like leaving ice cubes on the counter.
3. **Learn About Investing (Coming Soon!)**: This is where we'll really dig into making your money work harder than inflation. Think of it as training your money to run faster than the inflation treadmill.

The Planning Ahead Game

Here's a mind-bending thought: When you're planning to buy something in the future, you need to think about future prices, not today's prices. Want to buy a car in three years? That $25,000 car might cost $27,000 or $28,000 by then. Planning for retirement in 30 years? You'll need way more money than you think because of inflation. It's like planning a road trip but knowing the gas stations will be farther apart than they are today. You need to pack extra fuel.

The Psychology of Inflation (Why It Messes With Your Head)

Inflation plays tricks on your brain. You might think:

- "I'm spending more because I'm being irresponsible"
- "Why can't I seem to save as much as I used to?"
- "Am I worse with money than my parents were?"

Nope! You're dealing with a economic reality that affects everyone. Your parents' first apartment might have cost $300/month, but they were also making $15,000 a year. Everything was proportionally smaller. Don't let inflation make you feel bad about your financial progress. Recognize it, plan for it, but don't let it mess with your confidence.

The Bottom Line (Your Inflation Reality Check)

Inflation is like the weather, it's always there, sometimes it's mild, sometimes it's intense, but you can't make it go away by complaining about it. You can only dress appropriately and plan accordingly. Your money will always face the challenge of inflation. The question isn't whether inflation will happen (it will), but whether you'll be ready for it.

Your Anti-Inflation Action Plan

- ✓ Review your budget annually (prices change, your budget should too)
- ✓ Don't hoard cash (some is good, too much is risky)
- ✓ Learn about investing (make your money work harder)
- ✓ Plan for future prices (not today's prices)
- ✓ Stay informed (know what inflation rates are doing)
- ✓ Don't panic (steady planning beats emotional decisions)

Final Thought

"Inflation is the silent pickpocket of the financial world. It won't mug you in an alley, but it will slowly empty your pockets while you're not looking. The best defense is staying aware and planning ahead."

Your money's buying power will change over time, that's just reality. But with the right knowledge and planning, you can stay ahead of inflation instead of letting it leave you behind. Think of it as a slow-motion race where preparation beats speed.

Let's End with a Laugh

Why did the dollar bill go to therapy? Because it was having an identity crisis; it used to be worth something, but now it's just going through some changes!

(*But seriously, don't let inflation give you financial anxiety. Understanding it is the first step to beating it. Your money might be worth less tomorrow, but your financial knowledge is worth more every day.*)

Chapter 7: Your Job — Don't Lose It!

"Your job is your money machine. Don't break it by being careless with the instruction manual."

The Golden Ticket Reality Check

Remember Charlie and the Chocolate Factory? Charlie found that golden ticket and his whole life changed. Well, your job is basically your golden ticket to financial stability. But here's the plot twist nobody talks about: getting the ticket is just the beginning. Keeping it? That's where the real story starts.

Your job isn't just a paycheck, it's your financial foundation, your credit score's best friend, and your family's safety net all rolled into one. Lose it, and it's like watching dominoes fall in slow motion: bills pile up, credit scores tank, and stress levels explode like a shaken soda bottle.

The "I'm Obviously Going to Keep My Job" Trap

You might be thinking, "*Come on, of course I'll work hard! I'm not going to get fired!*"

That's exactly what my friend Marcus thought. Smart guy, good worker, always got his tasks done. But he had one tiny problem: he treated punctuality like a flexible suggestion rather than a requirement.

"*Ten minutes late isn't a big deal,*" he'd say. "*I stay late sometimes to make up for it.*"

Here is what Marcus didn't realize: employers don't want the smartest person who shows up whenever they feel like it. They want someone they can count on. Reliability beats brilliance almost every time.

The Superhero Analogy That Changed Everything

Imagine a superhero who can save the world but only shows up when they're in the mood. Not very helpful when the city is under attack, right? That's how employers think about unreliable employees. You might be incredibly talented, but if you're not dependable, you're like a superhero with a habit of sleeping through emergencies.

Employers want their Clark Kent; someone who shows up consistently, does what they say they'll do, and doesn't make excuses when things go wrong. They want someone who solves problems instead of creating them.

The True Cost of Losing Your Job (It's Worse Than You Think)

Losing your job is like losing your financial umbrella in a thunderstorm. Everything gets wet, and fast:

The Immediate Panic

- No paycheck means scrambling to cover rent, groceries, and bills
- You might lose your health insurance (because that's often tied to employment)
- Your credit score starts taking hits when you can't make payments
- The Ripple Effect
- Stress affects your sleep, your relationships, and your ability to job hunt effectively
- You might have to take the first job that comes along, even if it's not ideal
- The gap in your resume starts raising questions with future employers
- The Hidden Costs
- Job hunting costs money (gas, new clothes, maybe professional resume help)
- You might need to relocate or retrain for new opportunities

- The emotional toll of rejection and uncertainty is real

The "Just 10 Minutes" Disaster Story

Let me tell you about Sarah, who learned this lesson the hard way. She was a great employee; creative, hardworking, well-liked by customers. But she had a chronic lateness problem. Not hours late, just 10-15 minutes here and there.

"*Traffic was bad,*" she'd say. Or "*My alarm didn't go off.*" Or "*I couldn't find parking.*"

Her manager gave her warnings. HR had conversations with her. But Sarah thought, "*I'm a good employee. They won't fire me over a few minutes.*"

One morning, Sarah was 30 minutes late because she'd hit snooze one too many times. When she walked in, her manager was waiting with a pink slip.

"*But I'm usually only 10 minutes late!*" Sarah protested.

"*And that's 10 minutes too many,*" her manager replied. "*We need someone we can count on.*"

Sarah spent the next four months job hunting. She maxed out her credit cards just to survive. That "*just 10 minutes*" cost her thousands of dollars and months of stress. The brutal truth? Employers notice everything, even the minutes. They're not being petty; they're running a business that depends on people showing up when they say they will.

Your Job Security Playbook

Want to keep your job and maybe even get promoted? Here's your game plan:

1. Master the Art of Showing Up

- Be early or exactly on time, every single day
- If you're running late, call ahead (don't just text)
- Have a backup plan for transportation
- Set multiple alarms if you're not a morning person
- 2. Take Pride in Your Work
- Do your tasks well, even the boring ones
- Ask questions if you're unsure (it shows you care)
- Go the extra mile occasionally (but don't burn yourself out)
- Take feedback as a gift, not an insult
- Be a Professional Human Being
- Be polite to everyone—customers, coworkers, cleaning staff
- Keep personal drama out of the workplace
- Don't gossip or complain constantly
- Dress appropriately for your workplace

4. Communicate Like an Adult

- If you're struggling with something, talk to your manager
- Don't wait until you're drowning to ask for help

- Be honest about mistakes (they usually find out anyway)
- Keep your boss informed about your progress

The Mind-Reading Myth

Here's something that might blow your mind: your boss isn't a mind reader. Shocking, right? If you're having trouble with a task, struggling with personal issues that affect your work, or feeling overwhelmed, your manager probably has no idea unless you tell them. Most managers would rather help a good employee improve than go through the hassle of hiring and training someone new. But they can't help if they don't know what's wrong.

The Job-Hopping Tightrope

Switching jobs for better pay or growth opportunities is totally normal and often smart. But there's a difference between strategic career moves and job-hopping like you're playing musical chairs.

Leaving a job every few months makes you look like someone who can't commit or gets bored easily. Employers want to invest in people who will stick around long enough to make that investment worthwhile.

The Sweet Spot: Commit to your role long enough to fully understand its responsibilities, make meaningful contributions, and build a positive track record. Even more valuable is adopting a professional mindset—continually developing your skills, growing within the organization, and becoming a reliable and indispensable resource. This dedication creates a powerful foundation that, while often unseen, will ultimately yield significant long-term rewards for both you and the company.

Building Your Professional Reputation (Your Career Credit Score)

Your workplace reputation is like your credit score; it takes time to build, but it can be destroyed in minutes. And just like your credit score, it follows you everywhere. People talk. Industries are smaller than you think. That manager you were rude to might end up working at your dream company. That coworker you threw under the bus might become your future boss.

Reputation Builders:

- Being reliable and honest
- Helping others when you can
- Taking responsibility for your mistakes
- Showing up with a positive attitude (even on bad days)
- Reputation Destroyers:
- Lying on your resume or job applications
- Being consistently late or absent

- Gossiping or creating drama
- Throwing colleagues under the bus

The Side Hustle Balance

Side hustles are fantastic for extra income, but they can become a problem if they interfere with your main job. Your employer is paying you to be present and productive during work hours.

If your side hustle makes you tired, distracted, or unavailable when your main job needs you, you're playing with fire. It's like juggling while riding a unicycle; impressive if you can pull it off, but the crash can be spectacular.

The Rule: Your side hustle should enhance your financial situation, not jeopardize it by putting your main job at risk.

The Tax Reality Check

Speaking of jobs, let's talk about taxes for a hot second. Your employer will withhold taxes from your paycheck, it's not optional. Check your pay stubs to understand what's being taken out and why.

If you have side hustles or freelance work, congratulations! You're now partially self-employed, which means you need to save money for taxes. The IRS doesn't care that nobody explained this to you. They just want their money.

Your Professional Survival Kit

Here are the habits that will keep you employed and potentially promotable:

- ✓ Show up on time, every single time (this can't be emphasized enough)
- ✓ Be respectful and professional (even when you don't feel like it)
- ✓ Communicate clearly and honestly (no one likes guessing games)
- ✓ Plan your transportation (have a backup plan for your backup plan)
- ✓ Take feedback seriously (it's usually trying to help you)
- ✓ Keep learning (skills that grow are careers that grow)
- ✓ Build relationships (people hire people they like and trust)

The Bottom Line

Your job is your ticket to financial freedom, but it's not a lifetime guarantee. The economy changes, companies restructure, and industries evolve. The best job security comes from being the kind of employee that companies fight to keep.

Think of your job as a relationship. You want to be the reliable partner who shows up, communicates well, and contributes to the success of the team. Be someone your employer would hate to lose.

Final Thought

"Your job is your financial foundation. Don't let small mistakes create big problems. Treat every day like you're auditioning for your next opportunity—because you are."

Let's End with a Laugh

Why don't employees ever win at hide and seek at work? Because someone's always watching the clock! (*But seriously, punctuality is everything. Your future self will thank you for mastering this simple but crucial life skill.*)

Chapter 8: Save for Retirement — Even If You're Young

"Future You is depending on Present You. Don't let them down."

The Time Travel Dilemma

Imagine you could time travel to 2065. You knock on the door of your future home and meet 65-year-old you. They invite you in for coffee, and you notice they're living in a tiny apartment, eating generic cereal, and their biggest entertainment is watching free TV.

"*Why didn't you save for retirement?*" you ask.

Future You sighs. "*I thought I had time. I was going to start saving when I made more money. I was going to catch up later. I thought Social Security would be enough.*"

Then Future You looks at you with tired eyes and says, "*Please don't make the same mistake I did.*"

Now imagine the opposite scenario. You knock on that same door in 2065, and Future You opens it with a huge smile. They're living comfortably, traveling, enjoying hobbies, and they look at you with gratitude.

"*Thank you,*" they say. "*Thank you for thinking about me when you were young. Those small contributions you made in your twenties? They changed everything.*"

Which Future You do you want to meet?

The "I'm Too Young" Trap

Let's be honest about what you're probably thinking:

- "I'm too young to worry about retirement!"
- "I'll start saving when I make more money."
- "I have bigger problems right now, like rent and student loans."
- "Retirement is like 40 years away—that's forever!"
- These thoughts are totally normal and completely wrong. Here's why:

The Math Doesn't Lie: Starting early is like getting a magical money multiplier. The earlier you start, the less you need to save each month because time does most of the heavy lifting.

The Lifestyle Creep Reality: When you make more money, you tend to spend more money. That "*extra*" money you think you'll have later often gets eaten up by a bigger apartment, nicer car, or just general lifestyle inflation.

The Procrastination Trap: If you don't build the saving habit now, you probably won't build it later. It's like saying you'll start exercising when you get older, it doesn't usually happen.

What Is Retirement, Really?

Retirement isn't just "*being old and not working.*" It's about having the freedom to choose how you spend your time without worrying about money. Think of it like this: Your working years are when you trade your time for money. Retirement is when you've saved enough money to buy your time back. Some people retire to travel. Others want to volunteer, start a passion project, or just spend more time with family. But here's the thing, all of these dreams require money.

The Inflation Monster Returns

Remember our friend inflation from Chapter 6? Well, it doesn't take a vacation during your working years. It's going to keep making things more expensive every single year until you retire. Let's say you spend $3,000 a month on living expenses today. In 40 years, with just 3% annual inflation, you'd need about $9,800 a month to maintain the same lifestyle. That's more than triple! This is why "*I'll figure it out later*" is such a Dangerous plan. Later-you won't just need today's money, they'll need tomorrow's more-expensive money.

The Magical Money Multiplier (Compound Interest)

Here is where retirement savings gets really interesting. When you save money in retirement accounts and invest it, you earn returns. Then those returns earn returns. It's like a snowball rolling down a hill, getting bigger and bigger.

Let's look at two friends: Early Eddie and Late Larry.

Early Eddie starts saving $200 a month at age 22. He saves for 10 years, then stops completely. Total contributed: $24,000.

Late Larry waits until age 32 to start saving. He saves $200 a month for 33 years until retirement. Total contributed: $79,200.

Who has more money at retirement, assuming a 7% annual return and both retire at the same age?

Plot twist: Early Eddie! Even though he contributed less than one-third of what Larry did, he ends up with more money because he started earlier.

This is the power of compound interest; Einstein supposedly called it the eighth wonder of the world. Time is literally money.

The Real-Life Example That'll Blow Your Mind

Let me tell you about twin sisters, Sarah and Emma. They're both 22, both make the same salary, but they have very different approaches to retirement saving.

Sarah starts immediately, saving $150 a month in her 401(k). She never increases this amount, just $150 a month for 43 years.

Emma decides to wait. She wants to enjoy her twenties and thirties. At 35, she panics about retirement and starts saving $400 a month.

At retirement (age 65), assuming a 7% annual return:

- Sarah has about $1.2 million
- Emma has about $650,000

Sarah saved $77,400 total. Emma saved $144,000 total. But Sarah has nearly twice as much money because she started 13 years earlier.

The moral? Starting early is like getting a magic money multiplier that nobody can take away from you.

Retirement Accounts: Your Financial Time Machine

The government actually wants you to save for retirement (shocking, right?). That's why they created special accounts with tax benefits.

401(k) – The Workplace Hero

You contribute money from your paycheck before taxes, which means you pay less in taxes now. The money grows tax-free until you retire.

The Golden Rule: Always contribute enough to get the full benefit.

IRA (Individual Retirement Account) - The Do-It-Yourself Option

You can open this yourself at any bank, credit union, or investment company.

- Traditional IRA: You might get a tax deduction now, but you'll pay taxes when you withdraw the money in retirement.
- Roth IRA: You pay taxes on the money now, but withdrawals in retirement are tax-free. This is often better for young people who are in lower tax brackets.

The "I'll Save When I Make More" Myth

This is probably the most Dangerous financial myth out there. Here's what really happens when you make more money:

- Your rent goes up (better neighborhood, bigger place)
- Your car payment goes up (nicer car, because you "deserve" it)
- Your food costs go up (more restaurants, better groceries)

- Your entertainment costs go up (better concerts, nicer vacations)
- Your shopping costs go up (better clothes, more stuff)

It's called lifestyle inflation, and it's a retirement killer. The extra money you think you'll have often gets absorbed by your new, more expensive lifestyle.

The Pizza Money Perspective

Here is a way to think about it: If you can afford to order pizza twice a month, you can afford to save for retirement.

Two large pizzas delivered a month cost about $60. Investing $60 monthly from age 22 to 65 with a 7% annual return grows to about $350,000.

That's right, skipping two pizzas a month could literally make you a third of a millionaire by retirement. Future You would probably trade all the pizza in the world for that kind of financial security.

The Social Security Reality Check

Some people think Social Security will take care of them in retirement. Here's the truth: Social Security was designed to be a supplement, not your entire retirement plan.

The average Social Security benefit is about $1,700 a month. Could you live on $1,700 a month? In today's dollars?

Now imagine trying to live on that amount in 40 years when everything costs more.

Social Security is like a financial safety net; it's good to have, but you don't want to plan your whole retirement around it.

Investing vs. Saving (The Growth Game)

Here is something important: just saving money won't build wealth fast enough to beat inflation. You need to invest it.

Saving is like planting seeds in a jar—they stay safe, but they don't grow.

Investing is like planting seeds in soil—there's some risk, but they have the potential to grow into something much bigger.

For retirement, you generally want to invest in things like:

- Stock market index funds (own a piece of many companies)
- Target-date funds (automatically adjust as you get closer to retirement)
- Diversified mutual funds (spread risk across many investments)

The "I Don't Know How to Invest" Solution

Good news: You don't need to become a Wall Street expert. Most retirement accounts offer simple options like target-date funds. You pick the fund with a date close to when you'll retire, and it automatically adjusts your investments as you get older. It's like having autopilot for your retirement savings, set it and forget it.

Starting Your Retirement Savings Journey

Here's your step-by-step game plan:

Step 1: Check 401k availability

Explore available retirement plan options and consider starting with a 401(k). Aim to contribute consistently to help build your retirement savings.

Step 2: Explore an IRA

If your job doesn't offer a retirement plan, or if you want to save more, explore an IRA. Many financial institutions make this easy.

Step 3: Start Small

Don't wait until you can afford to save $500 a month. Start with $25, $50, or $100. The habit is more important than the amount.

Step 4: Automate It

Set up automatic contributions so you don't have to think about it. Pay yourself first, before you pay anyone else.

Step 5: Increase Gradually

Every time you get a raise, increase your retirement contributions by at least half of the raise amount. You'll barely notice the difference, but Future You will be thrilled.

Your Retirement Savings Action Plan

- ✓ Find out about 401k retirement plan
- ✓ Open an IRA if you don't have a workplace plan
- ✓ Start with any amount (even $25 a month is a start)
- ✓ Automate your contributions (make it happen without thinking)
- ✓ Increase your savings with raises (pay Future You first)
- ✓ Don't touch the money (it's for retirement, not emergencies)
- ✓ Review and adjust annually (but don't obsess over daily fluctuations)

The Bottom Line

Retirement might seem like a distant planet, but it's a destination you're going to reach whether you're prepared or not. The question isn't whether you'll get old, it's whether you'll be financially comfortable when you do. Every dollar you save for retirement in your twenties is like planting a tree that will provide shade for decades. The best time to plant a tree was 20 years ago. The second-best time is today.

Final Thought

"You're not saving for retirement. You're saving for freedom. The freedom to choose how you spend your time when you're older. That freedom is worth starting today."

Let's End with a Laugh

Why don't retirees ever get stressed about money? Because they started saving when they were young and let compound interest do the heavy lifting!

(*Okay, that's more inspirational than funny, but the point stands—start now, and Future You will be laughing all the way to the bank.*)

Chapter 9: The Pros You Need — Your Financial Dream Team

"You don't have to know everything. You just need to know who to ask."

The Superhero Team Analogy

Remember The Avengers? Each hero had their own superpowers, and together they could handle any crisis. Your financial life needs the same approach; a team of professionals with different expertise who can help you navigate the complex world of money, taxes, and legal stuff. You wouldn't expect Iron Man to handle what Doctor Strange specializes in, right? Similarly, you shouldn't expect to master every aspect of personal finance on your own. The smart move is building a team of trusted professionals who can help you avoid costly mistakes and plan for success.

The "I'll Figure It Out Myself" Trap

Let's be real, you're probably thinking:

- "I'll just use an online tax services for my taxes."
- "I don't need insurance yet, I'm young and healthy."
- "Estate planning? I don't have an estate!"
- "Financial advisors are for rich people."

These thoughts are understandable but Dangerous. Here's why:

- The Hidden Cost of DIY: Sure, you might save money upfront by doing everything yourself. But one mistake; missed tax deductions, inadequate insurance, or poor investment choices can cost you thousands or tens of thousands of dollars.
- The Complexity Factor: Financial laws change constantly. Tax codes are updated. Insurance policies have fine print that would make a lawyer's head spin. Professionals stay updated on these changes so you don't have to.
- The Time Value: Your time is valuable. Learning everything yourself means less time for earning money, building relationships, or just enjoying life.

Meet Your Financial Dream Team

The CPA® (Certified Public Accountant) – Your Tax Superhero

"Your guide through the mind-bending maze of tax laws."

Think of your CPA® as your financial translator. They take the incomprehensible language of tax codes and turn it into plain English and more importantly, into money saved.

What They Actually Do:

- Prepare your tax returns (correctly, the first time)
- Find deductions and credits you didn't know existed
- Help you plan for major life changes (marriage, home buying, starting a business)
- Represent you if the IRS decides to audit you (because nobody wants to face that alone)
- Provide year-round tax advice, not just April panic help

The Real-Life Horror Story:

My friend Dan decided to save money by doing his own taxes. He had a side hustle selling stuff online and thought, "*How hard can it be?*" He used free software and felt pretty proud of himself.

Six months later, Dan got a letter from the IRS. He owed $3,000 in additional taxes plus penalties because he'd calculated his self-employment tax wrong. The "*free*" tax software ended up costing him more than a CPA® would have charged for five years. The kicker? A good CPA® would have found legitimate deductions Dan missed, probably saving him more than their fee.

When You Need One:

- Your tax situation isn't just a W-2 and standard deduction.
- You have side hustles or freelance income.
- You're self-employed.
- You want to buy a house or make major investments.
- You receive that dreaded IRS letter.
- You want peace of mind and potential tax savings.

The Investment Perspective: A good CPA® doesn't cost you money, they save you money. Their fee is usually offset by the deductions they find and the mistakes they help you avoid.

The Estate Attorney: Your Life Planning Superhero

"The person who makes sure your wishes are followed when you can't speak for yourself."

Estate planning isn't just for wealthy people with mansions and art collections. It's for anyone who wants to control what happens to their stuff and their life if they can't make those decisions themselves.

What Estate Planning Actually Covers:

- Who gets your belongings when you die
- Who makes medical decisions if you're incapacitated
- Who handles your finances if you can't
- Who takes care of your children if you're not around
- How to minimize taxes and legal hassles for your family

The Essential Documents:

1. Will: Your instruction manual for who gets what. Without one, your state's laws decide, and they might not align with your wishes.
2. Power of Attorney: Designates someone to handle your financial affairs if you can't. This isn't just for elderly people, accidents and illnesses can happen to anyone.
3. Healthcare Directive: Explains your wishes for medical care if you can't communicate them yourself. This prevents family disputes and ensures your values are respected.
4. The Sobering Reality Check: My cousin Lisa was 28, healthy, and single. She thought estate planning was something for "*old people.*" Then she was in a serious car accident and spent two weeks in a coma. Her parents had to go to court to get permission to make medical decisions and access her bank accounts to pay her bills. It was expensive, time-consuming, and stressful during an already difficult time.

A simple healthcare directive and power of attorney would have prevented all of that legal drama.

When You Need One:

- You have any assets you care about (car, bank accounts, investments)
- You have children
- You want specific people to make decisions for you
- You want to minimize family conflicts and legal costs
- You're getting married or divorced
- You own a business

The Peace of Mind Factor: Estate planning isn't about preparing to die, it's about preparing to live with the confidence that your wishes will be respected, and your loved ones will be protected.

The Insurance and Financial Advisor – Your Risk Management and Wealth Building Superheros

"Your guide to protecting what you have and growing what you want."

Insurance and financial advisors help you with two crucial aspects of money management: protecting yourself from financial disasters and building wealth for the future.

What They Do:

- Analyze your insurance needs (auto, health, life, disability, renters/homeowners).
- Help you understand investment options.

- Create financial strategies for your goals.
- Explain complex financial products in human language.
- Help you balance risk and reward.
- Keep you from making emotional financial decisions.

The Insurance Reality: Insurance isn't exciting. It's not fun to pay for. But it's like a financial airbag, you hope you never need it, but you'll be grateful it's there if you do.

The Types of Insurance Young Adults Might Need:

1. Auto Insurance: Required by law in most states, and for good reason. One accident without insurance can ruin your financial life.
2. Health Insurance: Medical bills are the #1 cause of bankruptcy in the US. You're not invincible, even if you feel like it.
3. Renters Insurance: Your landlord's insurance doesn't cover your stuff. For about $15-20 a month, you can protect most of your belongings.
4. Disability Insurance: What if you couldn't work due to illness or injury? This replaces part of your income.
5. Life Insurance: If anyone depends on your income, you need this. It's cheapest when you're young and healthy.

The Credentials: When searching for financial professionals, understanding their credentials matters. Look for:

Advanced Degrees: Many top advisors have relevant degrees like:

- M.B.A. (Master of Business Administration)
- M.S.F.P. (Master of Science in Financial Planning)
- M.S.R.M.I. (Master of Science in Risk Management & Insurance)
- Ph.D. (Philosophy Doctor) in financial fields like the above-mentioned.

These indicate serious academic preparation.

Professional Designations:

- CFP® (Certified Financial Planner®): A license to offer a comprehensive financial advice
- ChFC® (Chartered Financial Consultant®): Advanced training in financial strategy
- CLU® (Chartered Life Underwriter®): Expertise in life insurance and estate planning
- CPCU® (Chartered Property & Casualty Underwriter®): Specialized in property and casualty insurance
- WMCP® (Wealth Management Certified Professional®): Focused on wealth management strategies

- RICP® (Retirement Income Certified Professional®): Focused on helping retired folks to manage their retirement income

These designations require rigorous study, passing comprehensive exams, ongoing education, and adherence to ethical standards.

The "Cheap Insurance" Disaster Story: My friend Marcus wanted to save money on car insurance. He found the cheapest policy online; bare minimum coverage, no extras. He felt like a smart shopper.

Six months later, Marcus rear-ended someone at a red light. His cheap insurance covered the other person's car repairs but not their medical bills or lost wages. Marcus ended up paying $15,000 out of pocket.

A professional insurance agent would have explained the risks and helped him find appropriate coverage that wouldn't have broken the bank but would have protected him from financial disaster.

How to Choose Your Financial Team

Red Flags to Avoid:

- Pressure to buy immediately.
- Promises of guaranteed high returns.
- Reluctance to explain things clearly.
- No verifiable credentials or licenses.
- Bad reviews or disciplinary actions.

- "Too good to be true" deals.

Green Flags to Look For:

- Patient explanations of complex topics.
- Transparent fees and costs.
- Proper licenses and credentials.
- Good references and reviews.
- Willingness to work with your budget.
- Focus on your goals, not their sales quotas.

Questions to Ask:

- What are your qualifications and credentials?
- How are you compensated?
- Can you provide references?
- What's your approach to my situation?
- How often will we review my plan?
- What happens if I need to make changes?

Building Professional Relationships

Think of your financial team as long-term relationships, not one-time transactions. Good professionals want to see you succeed because your success is their success.

1. Start Early: Don't wait until you're in crisis mode to build these relationships. It's easier to get good advice when you're not desperate.

2. Be Honest: Your professionals can only help you if they know your real situation. Don't hide debts, income, or goals.

3. Ask Questions: No question is too basic. Good professionals love educated clients who understand their recommendations.

4. Review Regularly: Your life changes, and your financial strategy should change with it. Annual reviews keep everyone on the same page.

The Investment in Professional Help

Yes, professional advice costs money. But think of it as an investment, not an expense. The right professional can:

- Save you more in taxes than they cost in fees.
- Help you avoid costly mistakes.
- Find opportunities you would have missed.
- Give you peace of mind.
- Save you time and stress.

Your Professional Team Action Plan

✓ Research and interview potential team members (don't just pick the first person you meet)

✓ Verify credentials and check references (a few minutes of research can save you from problems)

✓ Start with your most pressing needs (you don't need to hire everyone at once)

✓ Build relationships gradually (trust develops over time)

- ✓ Review and update regularly (your needs will change as your life changes)
- ✓ Don't be afraid to ask questions (understanding is empowering)
- ✓ Keep good records (make your professionals' jobs easier)

The Bottom Line

You don't need to become an expert in everything financial. But you do need to know who the experts are and when to ask for help.

Think of your financial team as the foundation of your financial house. You want that foundation to be solid, built by professionals who know what they're doing, and maintained by people you trust.

The money you spend on professional advice is some of the best money you'll ever spend. It's an investment in your financial future and your peace of mind.

Final Thought

"You're the CEO of your financial life. But every good CEO has a team of experts to help them make the best decisions. Build your team before you need them, and they'll help you avoid the mistakes that could cost you thousands."

Let's End with a Laugh

Why did the accountant break up with the calculator? Because they realized they needed someone they could truly count on for more than just numbers! (*But seriously, the right financial team is worth their weight in gold, or at least in the money they'll save you over the years.)*

Chapter 10: Conclusion — Habits to Win the Money Game

"If you read nothing else, read this. These habits will build your financial fortress brick by brick."

Congratulations! You've just completed a crash course in adulting that your high school guidance counselor probably should have taught you between algebra and dodgeball. You've journeyed through the wild, wonderful, and sometimes terrifying world of money, from credit scores that judge you harder than your mother-in-law, to retirement accounts that seem as mysterious as why people still use fax machines.

Here's the plot twist: The secret isn't knowing everything. It's doing a few simple things consistently.

Think of Money Like Your Garden (But Less Muddy)

Picture this: Money is like a garden. Without good habits, your financial garden looks like my neighbor Bob's yard; full of weeds, random shopping receipts blowing around, and that one credit card statement he's been avoiding since 2019. But with the right habits? You'll grow a lush, thriving money forest that not only looks impressive but actually feeds your dreams for years. Plus, you won't have to explain to anyone why there's a lawn gnome wearing a "YOLO" t-shirt in your front yard.

Why Habits Beat Magic (Sorry, Harry Potter)

Here is the brutal truth: There's no magic wand for money. No instant millionaire pill you can buy from that sketchy late-night infomercial. No foreign prince is going to email you with a fortune (trust me, I've been waiting since 2003).

But habits? They're like the slow cooker of success. Remember when your aunt discovered slow cookers and suddenly every family gathering featured mysteriously tender pot roast? That's what good financial habits do; they work quietly in the background, transforming your money situation from "ramen noodles for dinner again" to "I can actually afford the name-brand cereal."

You don't have to be a financial guru or understand why cryptocurrency exists. You just need to do a few key things consistently. Like brushing your teeth, but for your wallet. And significantly less minty fresh.

The Unrefutably Good Money Habits (Yes, That's a Real Word)

Based on everything we've covered, and trust me, we've covered more ground than a marathon runner with commitment issues; here are the core habits that will give you a rock-solid financial foundation:

1. Pay Your Bills On Time (Your Credit Score's Love Language)

Late payments are like showing up to a first date in pajamas. Technically possible, but it sends the wrong message. Your credit score notices everything, and it has an elephant's memory and a teenager's mood swings.

The Reality Check: Remember Sarah from Chapter 2? She paid her credit card a day late once and watched her interest rate jump faster than a cat seeing a cucumber. Don't be like Sarah. Set up automatic payments like you're running a small financial empire, because you are.

Pro tip: Your credit score is like a golden retriever; train it well with consistent payments, and it'll be loyal forever.

Neglect it, and it might chew up your chances of getting that dream apartment.

2. Keep Track of Your Money (GPS for Your Wallet)

You wouldn't drive cross-country without GPS (unless you enjoy explaining to your passengers why you're suddenly in Ohio when you were heading to Florida). So why would you navigate your finances blind?

Use your bank app, try budgeting tools, or go old-school with a notebook, whatever works for your brain. The point is knowing what's coming in and what's sneaking out like a teenager after curfew.

Real Talk: My friend Mike thought tracking expenses was "too much work" until he discovered he was spending $400 a month on coffee and convenience store snacks. That's a small car payment, folks. Knowledge is power, and power is not accidentally funding a 7-Eleven empire.

3. Build Your Emergency Fund (Your Financial Superhero Cape)

Life throws curveballs like a pitcher who's had too much caffeine. Your car breaks down, your laptop decides to become modern art, or your cat somehow needs emergency surgery (don't ask how they got into the neighbor's paint supplies).

Your emergency fund is your financial superhero cape. Start with $500; that's like 50 fancy coffees or one moderately dramatic vet visit. Then build up to 3-6 months of expenses. Keep it in a separate account so you're not tempted to "borrow" from it for that really cool gadget you saw online at 2 AM.

4. Get the Right Insurance (Your Financial Umbrella Collection)

Insurance is like owning multiple umbrellas; seems excessive until you're caught in a downpour wearing your best shoes. Health, auto, renters/homeowners, life, and disability insurance protect you from disasters that could financially flatten you like a pancake.

Story Time: My cousin Dan thought insurance was "just another bill" until a fender-bender turned into a $8,000 reality check. Now he's the guy who reads the fine print and actually knows what his deductible means.

Yes, insurance premiums feel like paying for a gym membership you never use. But when you need it, you'll be grateful you didn't skip it to save for that vintage record collection.

5. Start Retirement Saving Early (Future You is Watching)

Time is your financial superpower, and compound interest is basically magic that actually works. Starting to save at 25 versus 35 can mean the difference between “comfortable retirement” and “working at a supermarket because you have to.”

Even $25 a month beats waiting until you feel "ready." **Spoiler alert:** Nobody ever feels ready. It's like waiting for the perfect time to have kids or learn to parallel park, if you wait for perfect conditions, you'll be waiting forever.

The Math is Stunning: Save $50 monthly starting at age 25, and assuming a 7% return, you'll have about $175,000 at retirement. Start at 35? You'll have about $87,000. That's the power of giving your money time to do pushups.

6. Don't Spend Money You Don't Have (Revolutionary Concept)

Your checking account is not a magical portal to infinite funds, despite what your debit card might suggest at 2 AM when you're shopping online. Overdraft fees are like paying extra for the privilege of having no money, it's adding insult to financial injury.

Brutal Truth: That $35 overdraft fee for buying a $4 coffee is basically a 875% interest rate. Even loan sharks think that's excessive.

Treat your debit card like you would treat your grandmother's china; with respect, careful handling, and the understanding that breaking it will result in consequences nobody wants to deal with.

7. Understand Inflation (The Silent Money Ninja)

Inflation is like that friend who gradually eats all your fries; you don't notice until your plate is empty. Prices go up, your money's buying power goes down, and suddenly your dollar is working part-time when you need it to be full-time.

Combat inflation by saving and investing smartly. Your money sitting in a low-interest savings account is slowly losing the race against rising prices. It's like entering a marathon wearing flip-flops; technically possible, but you're making it unnecessarily difficult.

8. Be the Employee People Actually Want to Keep

Your job is your primary money machine, so don't treat it like that exercise bike gathering dust in your garage. Show up on time (crazy concept, right?), do quality work, and communicate with your boss when you need help.

Career Reality: It's exponentially easier and less stressful to keep your current job than to explain to your rent why you're suddenly between careers. Plus, job hunting is like dating; exhausting, full of rejection, and you have to pretend to be interested in things you're not.

Be reliable, be pleasant to work with, and remember that your reputation is like your browser history, it follows you everywhere and matters more than you think.

9. Use the Professionals (They're Like GPS for Your Money)

CPA®s, estate attorneys, insurance and financial advisors are your financial GPS system. Sure, you could navigate alone using stars and intuition, but why make life harder than necessary?

Reality Check: That tax mistake you made trying to save $200 on professional help? It just cost you $2,000 in penalties. Sometimes being cheap is expensive, like buying bargain parachutes or discount sushi.

Don't be afraid to ask for professional help. It's like having a translator in a foreign country; you might stumble through alone, but you'll get much better results with expert guidance.

10. Review and Adjust Your Plan Regularly (Financial Maintenance)

Your financial strategy needs regular maintenance like your car, your teeth, and your Netflix password security. Life changes faster than fashion trends, so your money strategy should adapt too.

Set a yearly "financial health checkup," review your budget, savings goals, insurance needs, and investment performance. Make adjustments like you're steering a ship through changing weather, not like you're desperately trying to fix something that's already broken.

The Power of Consistency (AKA The Tortoise Was Right)

These habits might seem as exciting as watching paint dry, but together and over time, they build unstoppable momentum. It's like compound interest for your entire financial life, small actions create massive results.

Think of it like going to the gym. Nobody gets abs from one workout, but consistent effort over time creates results that make people ask, "What's your secret?" The secret isn't sexy: it's showing up regularly and doing the work.

Your Money Story Starts Now

You now have the tools, knowledge, and habits to win the money game. Not by getting lucky or finding some secret loophole, but by building a solid foundation one smart decision at a time. Your future self is watching, hoping you'll make the choices today that lead to the life you want tomorrow. Don't let them down—they're counting on you to be the hero of your own financial story. Now go forth and prosper.

The next time life throws you a curveball, you will shift from saying, “Why didn’t you tell me before?” to confidently thinking, “I’ve read about this!”

Discover More from Jose Rosario

Thank you for reading this book.
If you'd like to explore my full collection, access exclusive content, and stay connected with future releases, visit my official landing page:
Scan the QR code or visit:
www.lumenarcenterprises.com

There you'll find:

- My complete book collection
- Bonus content not available on Amazon
- Early access to new releases
- Special reader resources
- Behind-the-scenes insights

You can also visit my Amazon Author Page:
www.amazon.com/author/joserosario

Your support means everything.
Thank you for being part of this journey.

—Jose Rosario

LUMENARC
ENTERPRISES

Made in United States
Troutdale, OR
11/03/2026

56852686R00086